GREAT
BIG
KNITS

GREAT BIG KNITS

Over twenty designer patterns

DAWN FRENCH
SYLVIE SOUDAN

Trafalgar Square Publishing

NORTH POMFRET, VERMONT

First published in the United States of America in 1993
by Trafalgar Square Publishing, North Pomfret, Vermont 05053

First published in Great Britain by Ebury Press

Editor **Sally Harding**
Designer **Bet Ayer**
Knitting Pattern Checker **Marilyn Wilson**
Knitting Charts **Textype**
Diagrams **Sally Harding**
Photographer **Trevor Leighton**
Models **Jane Crossley, Dawn French and Sharon Henry**
Stylist **Sharon Lewis**
Hair **Rick Haylor at John Frieda, assisted by Lesley Drummond**
Make-up **Charlie Duffy**
Photographer's Assistant **Ruth Crafer**

ISBN 0 943955 61 0
Library of Congress Catalog Card Number 92–64049

Phototypeset by Textype Typesetters, Cambridge
Printed and bound in Italy by New Interlitho S.p.a., Milan

CONTENTS

INTRODUCTION

So, another knitwear book . . . is this great or what?

Please don't think for one second that the reason we're doing a second book of these fabulous sweaters has anything to do with the thunderously huge response we had to the first one.

    Nor would I like you to believe that Sylvie designed loads more wonderful woollies that we just couldn't resist.

    Nor is the existence of this book in any way related to a huge upsurge of big women wanting to have a more positive self-image in recent years . . .

No. This book exists because of the following:

1. I was paid a full 50 dollars for the photo sessions (eat your heart out Christie Evangelista!)
2. I was allowed to keep all lipsticks used at the photo sessions, even the ones that didn't suit me.
3. I was permitted to graze at a table of mouthwatering goodies *all* day while shooting the photos.

I hope you enjoy this book as much as the last one, if not more, and I hope it gives you the kind of delicious pleasure it gave me to do it.

DAWN FRENCH
1992

MATISSE LADY

SIZE
One size only (see page 107 for choosing size)
Finished measurement around bust 146cm (58½")
See diagram for finished measurements of back, front and sleeves. To lengthen or shorten back and front, or sleeves see page 107.

MATERIALS
Rowan *Handknit DK Cotton*
20 x 50g (1¾oz) balls in Black (shade no. 252) A
3 x 50g (1¾oz) balls Bleached White (shade no. 263) B
One pair each 3¼mm (US size 3) and 4mm (US size 6) needles *or size to obtain correct tension (gauge)*

TENSION (GAUGE)
20 sts and 28 rows to 10cm (4") over st st on 4mm (US size 6) needles
Check your tension (gauge) before beginning.

NOTES
Do not strand yarn across back of work, but use a separate length of yarn for each isolated area of colour, twisting yarns at back when changing colours to avoid holes.
Read charts from right to left for RS (knit) rows and from left to right for WS (purl) rows.

BACK
Using smaller needles and yarn A, cast on 146 sts.
Beg K2, P2 rib as foll:
1st rib row P1, *K2, P2, rep from * to last st, K1.
Rep last row until ribbing measures 5cm (2") from beg, ending with a WS row.**
Change to larger needles and beg with a K row, work 164 rows in st st, so ending with a WS row.
Cast (bind) off 50 sts at beg of next 2 rows.
Slip rem 46 sts onto a st holder for back neck.

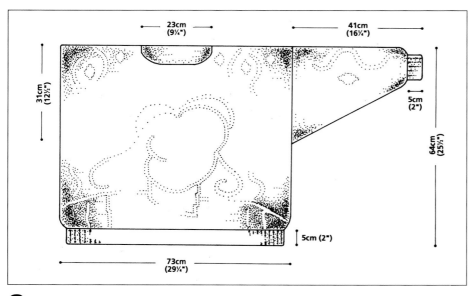

I'm going to get my mum to knit this one for me – I really love it.

FRONT

Work as for Back to **.
Change to larger needles and beg with first chart row (K row), work in st st foll chart for Front (see *Notes* above) until 146th chart row has been completed, so ending with a WS row.

Shape Neck

Beg neck shaping on next row as foll:

147th chart row (RS) Work 63 sts in patt, turn leaving rem sts on a spare needle.

Working on first side of neck only and cont to foll chart for patt throughout, cast (bind) off 3 sts at beg of next row and foll alt row, cast (bind) off 2 sts at beg of 2 foll alt rows, then dec one st at neck edge on 3 foll alt rows, so ending with a WS row. 50 sts.
Work 4 rows without shaping.
Cast (bind) off.

Return to rem sts and with RS facing, slip centre 20 sts onto a st holder, rejoin yarn to rem sts and work in patt to end of row. Cont to foll chart for patt throughout, work one row without shaping.
Cast (bind) off 3 sts at beg of next row and foll alt row, cast (bind) off 2 sts at beg of 2 foll alt rows, then dec one st at neck edge on 3 foll alt rows, so ending with a RS row. 50 sts.
Work 4 rows without shaping.
Cast (bind) off.

SLEEVES

Using smaller needles and yarn A, cast on 50 sts.
Work 5cm (2") in K2, P2 rib as for Back, ending with a WS row.
Change to larger needles and beg with a K row, work 2 rows in st st.
Cont in st st throughout, inc one st at each end of next row, so ending with a RS row. 52 sts.
Work one row without shaping.
Then beg with 5th chart row, foll chart for Sleeve *and at the same time* cont shaping Sleeve as before by inc one st at each end of every alt row until there are

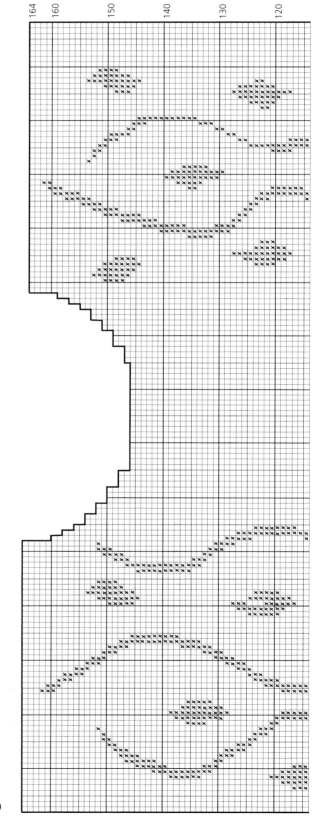

COLOUR KEY
☐ = A (Black)
☒ = B (Bleached White)

FRONT CHART

11

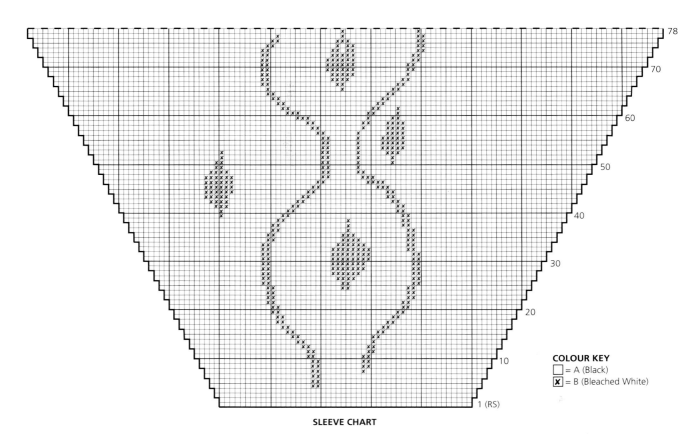

SLEEVE CHART

126 sts and ending with 78th chart row.
Using yarn A only, cont in st st without shaping until Sleeve measures 41cm (16¼") from beg, or desired length, ending with a WS row.
Cast (bind) off all sts.
Make the 2nd Sleeve in the same way as the first.

COLLAR
Press pieces lightly on WS with a warm iron over a damp cloth, omitting ribbing.
Join right shoulder seam.
Using smaller needles and yarn A and with RS facing, pick up and K22 sts down left front neck, K20 sts from front neck st holder, pick up and K22 sts up right front neck and K46 sts from back neck st holder. 110 sts.
Work 10cm (4") in K2, P2 rib as for Back, ending with a WS row.
Cast (bind) off in rib.

FINISHING
Join left shoulder seam and collar.
Placing centre of cast (bound) off sleeve edge at shoulder seam, sew Sleeves to Back and Front, matching sides.
Join side and sleeve seams.
Press seams lightly on WS with a warm iron over a damp cloth.

FOLK YOKE

SIZE

One size only (see page 107 for choosing size)
Finished measurement around bust 150cm (60")
See diagram for finished measurements of back, front and sleeves. To lengthen or shorten back and front, or sleeves see page 107.

MATERIALS

Rowan *Handknit DK Cotton*
19 x 50g (1¾oz) balls in Black (shade no. 252) A
5 x 50g (1¾oz) balls in Bleached White (shade no. 263) B
One pair each 3¼mm (US size 3) and 4mm (US size 6) needles *or size to obtain correct tension (gauge)*

TENSION (GAUGE)

20 sts and 28 rows to 10cm (4") over st st on 4mm (US size 6) needles
Check your tension (gauge) before beginning.

NOTES

When working border motifs along lower back and front, strand yarn A (black) loosely across back of work, but do not strand yarn B (white) across back of work. Instead use a separate length of yarn B for each isolated motif, twisting yarns at back when changing colours to avoid holes. When working the yoke motifs, strand yarn A as for the border, but strand yarn B only across the area of the patt. Read charts from right to left for RS (knit) rows and from left to right for WS (purl) rows.

BACK

Using smaller needles and yarn A, cast on 150 sts.
Beg K2, P2 rib as foll:
1st rib row P1, *K2, P2, rep from * to last st, K1.
Rep last row until ribbing measures 5cm (2") from beg, ending with a WS row.

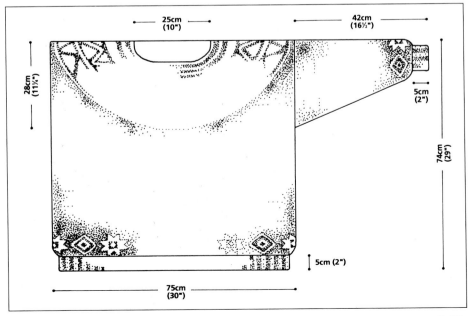

Very 60s, very 'ski', very nice.

BACK NECK

FRONT NECK

70

60

50

40

30

20

10

1 (RS)

YOKE CHART

18

10

1 (RS)

BORDER CHART FOR SLEEVE

COLOUR KEY
☐ = A (Black)
☒ = B (Bleached White)

15

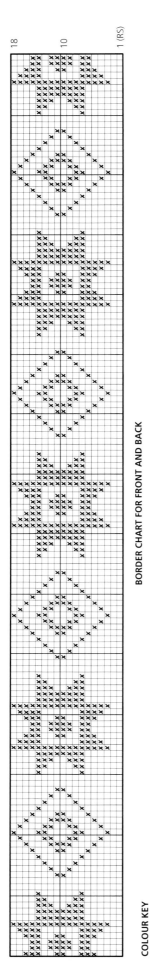

BORDER CHART FOR FRONT AND BACK

COLOUR KEY
☐ = A (Black)
☒ = B (Bleached White)

Change to larger needles and beg with a K row, work 2 rows in st st, so ending with a WS row. Cont in st st throughout and beg with 3rd chart row, foll chart for border (see *Notes* above) until 18th chart row has been completed, so ending with a WS row.

Using yarn A only, work 84 rows without shaping, ending with a WS row.**

Then beg with first chart row, foll chart (page 15) for yoke (see *Notes* above) until 70th chart row has been completed, so ending with a WS row.

Cast (bind) off 50 sts and break off yarn, slip centre 50 sts onto a st holder for back neck, then rejoin yarn and cast (bind) off rem 50 sts.

FRONT

Work as for Back to **.

Then beg with first chart row, foll chart for yoke until 50th chart row has been completed, so ending with a WS row.

Shape Neck

Beg neck shaping on next row as foll:

51st chart row (RS) Work 63 sts in patt, turn leaving rem sts on a spare needle.

Working on first side of neck only and cont to foll chart for patt throughout, cast (bind) off 2 sts at beg of next row and 4 foll alt rows, then dec one st at neck edge on 3 foll alt rows, so ending with a WS row. 50 sts.

Work 4 rows without shaping.

Cast (bind) off.

Return to rem sts and with RS facing, slip centre 24 sts onto a st holder, rejoin yarn to rem sts and work in patt to end of row.

Cont to foll chart for patt throughout, work one row without shaping.

Cast (bind) off 2 sts at beg of next row and 4 foll alt rows, then dec one st at neck edge on 3 foll alt rows, so ending with a RS row. 50 sts.

Work 3 rows without shaping.

Cast (bind) off.

SLEEVES

Using smaller needles and yarn A, cast on 50 sts.

Work 5cm (2") in K2, P2 rib as for Back, ending with a WS row.

Change to larger needles and beg with a K row, work 2 rows in st st.

Cont in st st throughout and beg with 3rd chart row, foll chart for sleeve border (page 15) *and at the same time* shape Sleeve by inc one st at each end of next and every foll alt row until 18th chart row has been completed. 66 sts.

Using yarn A only, cont inc one st at each end of every alt row until there are 112 sts.

Work without shaping until Sleeve measures 42cm (16½") from beg or desired length, ending with a WS row.

Cast (bind) off all sts.

Make the 2nd Sleeve in the same way as the first.

COLLAR

Press pieces lightly on WS with a warm iron over a damp cloth, omitting ribbing.

Join right shoulder seam.

Using smaller needles and yarn A and with RS facing, pick up and K22 sts down left front neck, K24 sts from front neck st holder, pick up and K22 sts up right front neck and K50 sts from back neck st holder. 118 sts.

Work 10cm (4") in K2, P2 rib as for Back, ending with a WS row.

Cast (bind) off in rib.

FINISHING

Join left shoulder seam and collar.

Placing centre of cast (bound) off sleeve edge at shoulder seam, sew Sleeves to Back and Front, matching sides.

Join side and sleeve seams.

Press seams lightly on WS with a warm iron over a damp cloth.

CIRCLE OF ONE

SIZE

One size only (see page 107 for choosing size)
Finished measurement around bust 158cm (63")
See diagram for finished measurements of back, front and sleeves. To lengthen or shorten back and front, or sleeves see page 107.

MATERIALS

Rowan *Handknit DK Cotton*
22 x 50g (1¾oz) balls in Black (shade no. 252) A
2 x 50g (1¾oz) balls in Bleached White (shade no. 263) B
One pair each 3¼mm (US size 3) and 4mm (US size 6) needles *or size to obtain correct tension (gauge)*

TENSION (GAUGE)

20 sts and 28 rows to 10cm (4") over st st on 4mm (US size 6) needles
Check your tension (gauge) before beginning.

NOTES

When working circle motif, do not strand yarn across back of work, but use a separate ball for each isolated area of colour, twisting yarns at back when changing colours to avoid holes. Read chart from right to left for RS (knit) rows and from left to right for WS (purl) rows.

BACK

Using smaller needles and yarn A, cast on 158 sts.
Beg K1, P1 rib as foll:
1st rib row *K1, P1, rep from * to end.
Rep last row until ribbing measures 13cm (5") from beg, ending with a WS row.**
Change to larger needles and beg with a K row, work in st st until Back measures 73cm (28¾") from beg, ending with a WS row.
Shape Neck
Cont in st st throughout, beg

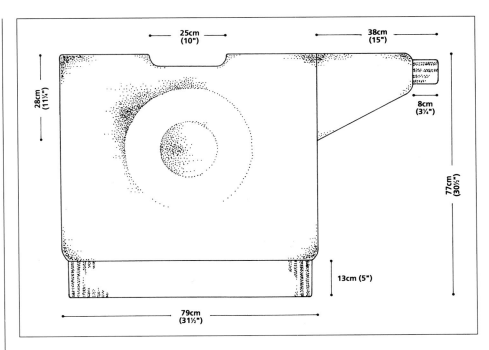

neck shaping on next row as foll:
Next row (RS) K60, turn leaving rem sts on a spare needle.
Working on first side of neck only, dec one st at neck edge on every row 4 times, then dec one st at neck edge on 2 foll alt rows. 54 sts.
Work 3 rows without shaping.
Cast (bind) off.
Return to rem sts and with RS facing, rejoin yarn, cast (bind) off centre 38 sts and K to end.
Complete 2nd side of neck to match first side, reversing all shaping.

FRONT

Work as for Back to **.
Change to larger needles and beg with a K row, work 12cm (4¾") in st st, ending with a WS row.
Place Motif
Begin circle motif (see *Notes* above) on next row as foll:
1st motif row (RS) K73, change to yarn B and K12, then with separate ball of yarn A K73.
2nd motif row (WS) P70 with yarn A, P18 with yarn B, P70 with yarn A.

The last 2 rows set the position of the circle motif on the Front of the sweater. Cont in st st, foll chart (page 18) for motif from 3rd chart row until the motif is complete, so ending with a WS row.
Using yarn A only, cont in st st throughout until there are the same number of rows as Back to neck shaping.
Shape neck and complete as for Back.

SLEEVES

Using smaller needles and yarn A, cast on 50 sts. Work 8cm (3¼") in K1, P1 rib as for Back, ending with a WS row.
Change to larger needles and beg with a K row, work in st st throughout *and at the same time* inc one st at each end of 3rd row and then every foll alt row until there are 112 sts, so ending with a RS row.
Work without shaping until Sleeve measures 38cm (15"), ending with a WS row.
Cast (bind) off all sts.
Make the 2nd Sleeve in the same way as the first.

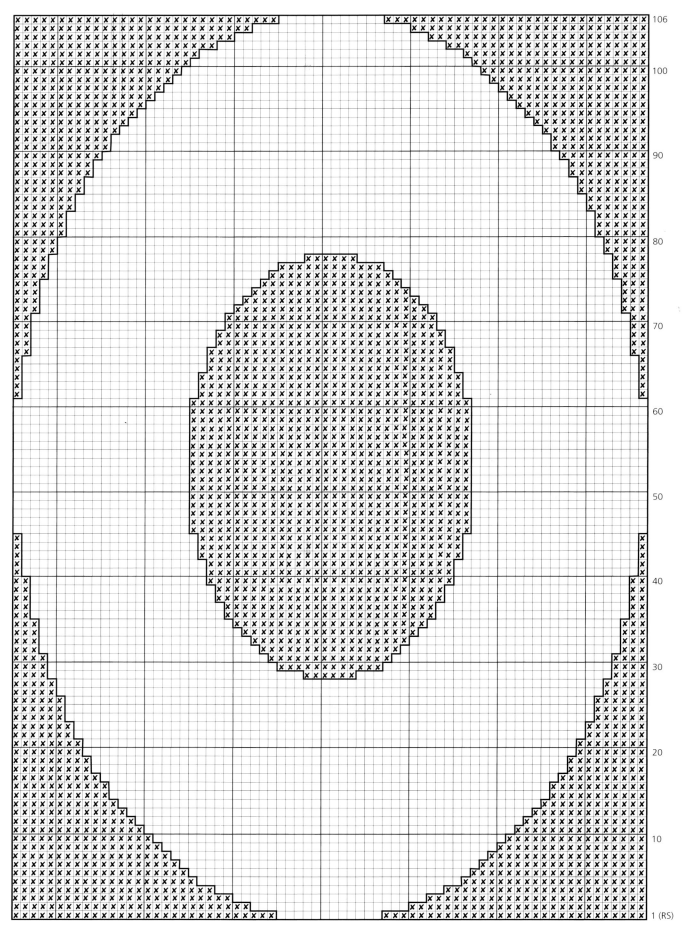

CIRCLE MOTIF CHART

A truly great jumper.

NECKBAND

Press pieces lightly on WS with a warm iron over a damp cloth, omitting ribbing.
Join right shoulder seam.
Using smaller needles and yarn A and with RS facing, pick up and K12 sts down left front neck, 38 sts across centre front, 12 sts up right front neck, 12 sts down right back neck, 38 sts across centre back neck and 12 sts up left back neck. 124 sts.
P one row. Then work 4cm (1½″) in K1, P1 rib.
Cast (bind) off in rib.

FINISHING

Join left shoulder seam and neckband.
Placing centre of cast (bound) off sleeve edge at shoulder seam, sew Sleeves to Back and Front, matching sides.
Join side and sleeve seams.
Press seams lightly on WS with a warm iron over a damp cloth.

COLOUR KEY
☐ = A (Black)
☒ = B (Bleached White)

Three sure-fire winners. I lusted after all three (not a pretty sight, I usually dribble when excited).

ARAN JACKET

SIZE

One size only (see page 107 for choosing size)
Finished measurement around bust 150cm (59¼")
See diagram for finished measurements of back, fronts and sleeves. To lengthen or shorten back and fronts, or sleeves see page 107.

MATERIALS

27 x 50g (1¾oz) balls (approx 65m or 71yd per ball) of a chunky (bulky) yarn in Cream
One pair each 5½mm (US size 9) and 6½mm (US size 10½) needles *or size to obtain correct tension (gauge)*
8 stitch markers (see *Notes*)

TENSION (GAUGE)

14 sts and 20 rows to 10cm (4") over st st on 6½mm (US size 10½) needles
Check your tension (gauge) before beginning.

NOTES

Several st patts are worked in panels across the Back, Fronts and Sleeves. The charts provided indicate the number of sts across the first row of each patt panel. Instructions are given for placing st markers between the panels. These st markers are slipped in each row so that they are always positioned on the needles between the panels as a guide for the knitter. An experienced knitter may not find the st markers necessary.

MOSS (SEED) ST

The foll instructions are for working moss (seed) st over an even number of sts.
1st row (RS) *K1, P1, rep from * to end.
2nd row *P1, K1, rep from * to end.
These 2 rows are repeated to form the moss (seed) st patt.

ZIGZAG PANEL

This panel is worked over 8 sts.
1st row (RS) P6, take RH needle in front of first st on LH needle and K the 2nd st, then P first st and slip both sts tog off LH needle — called *cross 2 right* or *C2R*.
2nd row and foll WS rows Purl.

3rd row P5, C2R, P1.
5th row P4, C2R, P2.
7th row P3, C2R, P3.
9th row P2, C2R, P4.
11th row P1, C2R, P5.
13th row C2R, P6.
15th row Take RH needle behind first st on LH needle and P the 2nd st tbl, then K first st and slip both sts tog off LH needle — called *cross 2 left* or *C2L* —, P6.
17th row P1, C2L, P5.
19th row P2, C2L, P4.
21st row P3, C2L, P3.
23rd row P4, C2L, P2.
25th row P5, C2L, P1.
27th row P6, C2L.
28th row P1, K7.
These 28 rows are repeated to form the zigzag patt.

LADDER PANEL

This patt is worked over 11 sts.
1st row (RS) P3, K5, P3.
2nd row K3, P5, K3.
3rd and 4th rows As first and 2nd rows.
5th row As first row.
6th row K11.
These 6 rows are repeated to form the ladder patt.

HERALDIC PANEL

Heraldic patt is worked over a multiple of 24 sts. On the Back this panel is worked over 48 sts and on the Fronts over 24 sts.
1st row (foundation row) (RS) Knit.
2nd row (WS) K2, P2, *K4, P2, rep from * to last 2 sts, K2.
3rd row K2, C2R (see zigzag patt), K4, C2L (see zigzag patt), *K4, C2R, K4, C2L, rep from * to last 2 sts, K2.
4th row As 2nd row.
5th row Knit.
6th row As 2nd row.
7th row As 3rd row.
8th row As 2nd row.
9th row K3, C2L, K2, C2R, *K6, C2L, K2, C2R, rep from * to last 3 sts, K3.
10th row (K2, P3) twice, *K4, P3, K2, P3, rep from * to last 2 sts, K2.

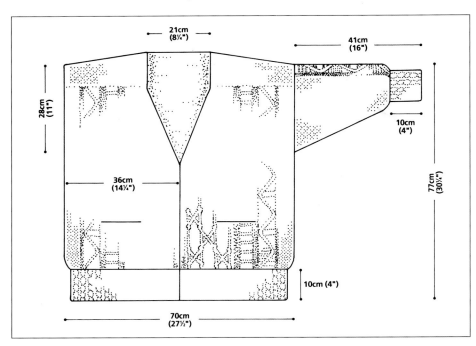

You can't beat a good cardi.

11th row K4, C2L, C2R, *K8, C2L, C2R, rep from * to last 4 sts, K4.

12th row K2, P8, *K4, P8, rep from * to last 2 sts, K2.

13th row K5, C2R, *K10, C2R, rep from * to last 5 sts, K5.

14th row As 12th row.

15th row K4, C2R, C2L, *K8, C2R, C2L, rep from * to last 4 sts, K4.

16th row As 10th row.

17th row K3, C2R, K2, C2L, *K6, C2R, K2, C2L, rep from * to last 3 sts, K3.

18th row As 2nd row.

19th row K2, C2L, K4, C2R, *K4, C2L, K4, C2R, rep from * to last 2 sts, K2.

20th row As 2nd row.

21st row Knit.

22nd row As 2nd row.

23rd row As 19th row.

24th row As 2nd row.

25th row K9, *C2L, K2, C2R, K6, rep from * to last 3 sts, K3.

26th row K2, P2, K4, *P3, K2, P3, K4, rep from * to last 4 sts, P2, K2.

27th row K10, *C2L, C2R, K8, rep from * to last 2 sts, K2.

28th row K2, P2, K4, *P8, K4, rep from * to last 4 sts, P2, K2.

29th row K11, *C2L, K10, rep from * to last st, K1.

30th row As 28th row.

31st row K10, *C2R, C2L, K8, rep from * to last 2 sts, K2.

32nd row As 26th row.

33rd row K9, *C2R, K2, C2L, K6, rep from * to last 3 sts, K3.
The 2nd-33rd rows are repeated to form the heraldic patt. (*Note:* Remember to beg each foll rep with 2nd row, omitting first row.)

BOX STITCH PATTERN
On the Back and Fronts (and the first row of the Sleeves) this st patt is worked over a multiple of 4 sts plus 2 extra.

1st row K2, *P2, K2, rep from * to end.

2nd row P2, *K2, P2, rep from * to end.

3rd row As 2nd row.

4th row As first row.
These 4 rows are repeated to form the box st patt.

BACK
Using smaller needles, cast on 106 sts.
Beg cable rib as foll:

1st rib row (RS) P1, *K2, P1, rep from * to end.

2nd rib row K1, *P2, K1, rep from * to end.

3rd rib row P1, *take RH needle behind first st on LH needle and K the 2nd st tbl, then K first st and slip both sts tog off LH needle, P1, rep from * to end.

4th rib row As 2nd row.
Rep last 4 rows until cable rib measures 10cm (4") from beg, ending with a 2nd rib row.
Change to larger needles and position patt sts across Back (see *Notes* and page 26) as foll:

1st patt row (RS) Work first row of moss (seed) st over first 8 sts and slip st marker onto RH needle; P2 and slip st marker onto RH needle; work first row of zigzag panel over next 8 sts and slip on st marker; work first row of ladder panel over next 11 sts and slip on st marker; work first row (foundation row) of heraldic patt over next 48 sts and slip on st marker; work first row of ladder panel over next 11 sts and slip on st marker; work first row of zigzag patt over next 8 sts and slip on st marker; P2 and slip on st marker; work first row of moss (seed) st over last 8 sts.

2nd patt row Work 2nd row of moss (seed) st over first 8 sts and slip marker; K2 and slip marker; work 2nd row of zigzag panel over next 8 sts and slip marker; work 2nd row of ladder panel over next 11 sts and slip marker; work 2nd row of heraldic patt over next 48 sts and slip marker; work 2nd row of ladder panel over next 11 sts and slip marker; work 2nd row of zigzag patt over next 8 sts and slip marker; K2 and slip marker; work 2nd row of moss (seed) st over last 8 sts.
Cont in patt as set (working moss st, zigzag, ladder and heraldic panels between markers foll row by row instructions, and working rem sts as set in first and 2nd patt rows above) until Back measures 68cm (26¾") from beg, ending with a WS row. This completes panels.
Work in box st patt until Back measures 77cm (30¼") from beg, ending with a WS row.

Shape Shoulders
Keeping box st patt correct throughout and casting (binding) off in patt, cast (bind) off 14 sts at beg of next 2 rows, then 12 sts at beg of next 4 rows.
Cast (bind) off rem 30 sts in patt for back neck.

LEFT FRONT
Before beg Left Front, make pocket lining.

Pocket Lining
Using larger needles, cast on 22 sts.
Work in st st until lining measures 15cm (6") from beg, ending with a WS (P) row.
Break off yarn and slip sts onto a st holder to be used later.

Begin Left Front
Using smaller needles, cast on 55 sts.
Work 10cm (4") in cable rib as for Back, so ending with a 2nd rib row and inc one st at side edge of last row. 56 sts.**
Change to larger needles and position patt sts across Left Front as foll:

1st patt row (RS) Work first row of moss (seed) st over first 8 sts and slip st marker onto RH needle; P2 and slip st marker onto RH needle; work first row of zigzag panel over next 8 sts and slip on st marker; work first row of ladder panel over next 11 sts and slip on st marker; work first row (foundation row) of heraldic patt over next 24 sts and slip on st marker; P3.

2nd patt row K3 and slip

marker; work 2nd row of heraldic patt over next 24 sts and slip marker; work 2nd row of ladder panel over next 11 sts and slip marker; work 2nd row of zigzag patt over next 8 sts and slip marker; K2 and slip marker; work 2nd row of moss (seed) st over last 8 sts.

Cont in patt as set until Left Front measures 25cm (10") from beg, ending with a WS row.

Place Pocket
***Keeping patt correct as set, place pocket on next row as foll:

Next row (RS) Work 17 sts in patt, slip next 22 sts onto a st holder, then with RS facing, work the 22 sts of the pocket lining in patt from the st holder, work in patt to end.***

Work in patt without shaping until Left Front measures 41cm (16") from beg, ending with a RS row.

Shape V-neck
****Cont in patt, dec one st at beg of next row (neck edge) and at neck edge on every foll 3rd row until there are 38 sts *and at the same time* when there are same number of rows as Back to box st, change to box st.****

Keeping box st patt correct, work rem 38 sts without shaping until there are same number of rows as Back to shoulder, ending with a WS row.

Shape Shoulder
Keeping to box st, cast (bind) off in patt 14 sts at beg of next row and 12 sts at beg of 2 foll alt rows.

RIGHT FRONT
Work as for Left Front to **.
Change to larger needles and position patt sts across Right Front as foll:

1st patt row (RS) P3 and slip st marker onto RH needle; work first row (foundation row) of heraldic patt over next 24 sts and slip on st marker; work first row of ladder panel over next 11 sts and slip on st marker; work first

row of zigzag patt over next 8 sts and slip on st marker; P2 and slip on st marker; work first row of moss (seed) st over last 8 sts.

2nd patt row Work 2nd row of moss (seed) st over first 8 sts and slip marker; K2 and slip marker; work 2nd row of zigzag panel over next 8 sts and slip marker; work 2nd row of ladder panel over next 11 sts and slip marker; work 2nd row of heraldic patt over next 24 sts and slip marker; K3.

Cont in patt as set until there are same number of rows as Left Front to pocket, so ending with a WS row.

Place Pocket
Work as for Left Front from *** to ***.

Work in patt without shaping until Right Front measures same

as Left Front to neck shaping, ending with a WS row.

Shape V-neck
Work as for Left Front from **** to ****.

Keeping box st patt correct, work rem 38 sts without shaping until there are same number of rows as Back to shoulder, ending with a RS row.

Shape Shoulder
Shape shoulder as for Left Front.

SLEEVES
Using smaller needles, cast on 55 sts.

Work 10cm (4") in cable rib as for Back, ending with a 2nd rib row and inc one st at end of last row. 56 sts.

Change to larger needles and position the patt sts across the Sleeve as foll:

1st patt row (RS) Work first row of box st patt over first 22 sts and slip st marker onto RH needle; P2 and slip on st marker; work first row of zigzag panel over next 8 sts and slip on st marker; P2 and slip on st marker; work first row of box st patt over last 22 sts.

2nd patt row (WS) Work 2nd row of box st patt over first 22 sts and slip marker; K2 and slip marker; work 2nd row of zigzag panel over next 8 sts and slip marker; K2 and slip marker; work 2nd row of box st patt over last 22 sts.

Cont in patt as set, inc one st at each end of next row and every foll alt row until there are 82 sts *and at the same time* work all extra sts outside first and last st marker in box st patt.

Work in patt without shaping until Sleeve measures 41cm (16")

from beg or desired length, ending with a WS row.
Cast (bind) off all sts in patt.
Make the 2nd Sleeve in the same way as the first.

COLLAR

Do not press.
Join shoulder seams.
Using smaller needles, cast on 14 sts.
Work in moss (seed) st until Collar, when slightly stretched, fits up centre edge of Right Front from cast-on edge to neck shaping.
Keeping moss (seed) st correct throughout, inc one st at beg of next row and at same edge on every foll 4th row until there are 32 sts.
Work without shaping until Collar reaches centre back neck.
Cast (bind) off in patt.

Work the 2nd half of the Collar in exactly the same way.

FINISHING

Sew the Collar pieces to Fronts, with increased edges to neck edges. Join collar seam at centre back neck.

Pocket Top

Using smaller needles and with RS of Left Front facing, work in cable rib as for Back across 22 sts from st holder at pocket top.
Work 5cm (2") in cable rib. Cast (bind) off in rib.
Work pocket top on Right Front in the same way. Sew pocket linings neatly to WS of Fronts. Sew ends of pocket tops to RS. Placing centre of cast (bound) off sleeve edge at shoulder seam, sew Sleeves to Back and Fronts, matching sides.
Join side and sleeve seams.

STITCH PATTERNS ACROSS ARAN JACKET BACK

moss (seed) st	rev st st	zigzag panel	ladder panel	heraldic panel	ladder panel	zigzag panel	rev st st	moss (seed) st	
8	2	8	11	48	11	8	2	8	sts

STITCH PATTERNS ACROSS ARAN JACKET LEFT FRONT

rev st st	heraldic panel	ladder panel	zigzag panel	rev st st	moss (seed) st	
3	24	11	8	2	8	sts

STITCH PATTERNS ACROSS ARAN JACKET RIGHT FRONT

moss (seed) st	rev st st	zigzag panel	ladder panel	heraldic panel	rev st st	
8	2	8	11	24	3	sts

STITCH PATTERNS ACROSS ARAN JACKET SLEEVES

box st	rev st st	zigzag panel	rev st st	box st	
22	2	8	2	22	sts

FISHERMAN'S RIB

SIZE
One size only (see page 107 for choosing size)
Finished measurement around bust 162cm (64½")
See diagram for finished measurements of back, front and sleeves. To lengthen or shorten back and front, or sleeves see page 107.

MATERIALS
36 x 50g (1¾oz) balls of Jaeger *Sport* in Cream (shade no. 220)
One pair each 4mm (US size 6) and 4½mm (US size 7) needles *or size to obtain correct tension (gauge)*

TENSION (GAUGE)
17 sts and 38 rows to 10cm (4") over fisherman's rib patt (slightly stretched) on 4½mm (US size 7) needles
Check your tension (gauge) before beginning.

BACK
Using smaller needles, cast on 138 sts.
Beg K2, P2 rib as foll:
1st rib row (RS) P2, *K2, P2, rep from * to end.
2nd rib row K2, *P2, K2, rep from * to end.
Rep last 2 rows until ribbing measures 8cm (3¼") from beg, ending with a WS row and decreasing one st at end of last row. 137 sts.
Change to larger needles and K one row.
Then beg fisherman's rib patt as foll:
1st patt row (WS) Sl 1, *K next st in the row below and slip st above it off the LH needle, P1, rep from * to end.
2nd patt row (RS) Sl 1, *P1, K next st in the row below and slip st above it off the LH needle, rep from * to last 2 sts, P1, K1.
Rep last 2 rows until Back measures 74cm (29") from beg, ending with a WS row.
Keeping to patt as set, cast (bind)
off 48 sts (in patt) at beg of next 2 rows.
Cast (bind) off rem 41 sts in patt for back neck.

FRONT
Work as for Back until Front measures 67cm (26¼") from beg, ending with a WS row.
Shape Neck
Beg neck shaping on next row as foll:
Next row (RS) Work 57 sts in patt, turn leaving rem sts on a spare needle.
Keeping patt correct throughout and working on first side of neck only, dec one st at neck edge on next and every foll row 4 times in all, then dec one st at neck edge on 5 foll alt rows. 48 sts.
Work without shaping until there are same number of rows as Back to shoulder, ending at side edge.
Cast (bind) off in patt.
Return to rem sts and with RS facing, rejoin yarn and cast (bind) off centre 23 sts in patt, then work in patt to end of row.
Complete 2nd side of neck to match first side, reversing all shaping.

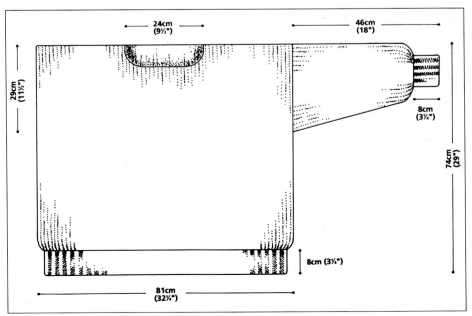

SLEEVES

Using smaller needles, cast on 62 sts.
Work 8cm (3¼") in K2, P2 rib as for Back, ending with a WS row and dec one st at end of last row. 61 sts.
Change to larger needles and K one row.
Work in fisherman's rib patt as for Back *and at the same time*, keeping patt correct as set, inc one st at each end of 7th row and then every foll 6th row until there are 99 sts.
Work in patt without shaping until Sleeve measures 46cm (18") from beg or desired length, ending with a WS row.
Cast (bind) off all sts very loosely in patt.
Make the 2nd Sleeve in the same way as the first.

COLLAR

Using smaller needles, cast on 129 sts. K one row.
Work in fisherman's rib patt as for Back for 8cm (3¼"), ending with a RS row.
Change to larger needles and cont in patt as set until Collar measures 20cm (8") from beg.
Cast (bind) off very loosely in patt.

FINISHING

Do not press.
Join shoulder seams.
Sew sides of collar tog.
Place collar seam at centre back neck, with RS of Collar facing WS of Back, and evenly sew cast-on edge of Collar to sweater along neck edge.
Placing centre of cast (bound) off sleeve edge at shoulder seam, sew Sleeves to Back and Front, matching sides.
Join side and sleeve seams.
Fold Collar to RS.

Roomy enough to fit a couple of fishermen in with you. This is one of my favourites – to die for!

HALF AND HALF

SIZES

To choose appropriate size see page 107
Finished measurement around bust 128[154]cm (51½[61½]")
Figures for larger size are given in brackets []; where there is only one set of figures, it applies to both sizes.
See diagram for finished measurements of back, front and sleeves. To lengthen or shorten back and front, or sleeves see page 107.

MATERIALS

Rowan *Handknit DK Cotton*
10[12] x 50g (1¾oz) balls in Ecru (shade no. 251) A
10[12] x 50g (1¾oz) balls in Bathstone (shade no. 257) or Black (shade no. 252) B
One pair each 4mm (US size 6) and 4½mm (US size 7) needles *or size to obtain correct tension (gauge)*

TENSION (GAUGE)

19 sts and 25 rows to 10cm (4") over st st on 4½mm (US size 7) needles
Check your tension (gauge) before beginning.

NOTES

This sweater can be worked in either of the two colourways shown and with either of the two neck styles shown — crewneck or turtleneck. The neck shaping for the Back and Front is worked exactly the same for the crewneck and the turtleneck. When knitting the Back and Front, use a separate ball of yarn for each side of the work, twisting yarns at back when changing colours at the centre of each row to avoid holes.

BACK

Using smaller needles and yarn A, cast on 61[73] sts, then change to yarn B and cast on 61[73] sts, so that a total of 122[146] sts have been cast on.
Changing colour in the middle of each row (see *Note* above) so that all sts cast on in B are worked in B and all sts cast on in A are worked in A, beg K1, P1 rib as foll:
1st rib row (RS) Using yarn B, (K1, P1) 30[36] times, K1, then change to yarn A and work (P1, K1) to last st, P1.
2nd rib row Using yarn A, (K1,

P1) 30[36] times, K1, then change to yarn B and work (P1, K1) to last st, P1.
Rep last 2 rib rows until ribbing measures 6cm (2½") from beg, ending with a WS row.
Change to larger needles and beg with a K row, cont to change colour in the middle of each row and work in st st until Back measures 74[79]cm (29[31]") from beg, ending with a WS row.
Cast (bind) off 38[50] sts at beg of next 2 rows.
Slip rem 46 sts onto a st holder for back neck.

FRONT

Using smaller needles and yarn B, cast on 61[73] sts, then change to yarn A and cast on 61[73] sts, so that a total of 122[146] sts have been cast on.
Changing colour in the middle of each row (see *Notes* above) so that all sts cast on in A are worked in A and all sts cast on in B are worked in B, beg K1, P1 rib as foll:
1st rib row (RS) Using yarn A, (K1, P1) 30[36] times, K1, then change to yarn B and work (P1, K1) to last st, P1.
2nd rib row Using yarn B, (K1, P1) 30[36] times, K1, then change to yarn A and work (P1, K1) to last st, P1.
Rep last 2 rib rows until ribbing measures 6cm (2½") from beg, ending with a WS row.
Note: As you can see, the colours are reversed on the Back and Front so that when the Back and Front are sewn tog at the side seams the colours will match.
Change to larger needles and beg with a K row, cont to change colour in the middle of each row and work in st st until Front measures 63[68]cm (24½[26½]") from beg, ending with a WS row.
Shape Neck
Working in st st throughout, beg neck shaping on next row as foll:
Next row (RS) Using A, K51[63],

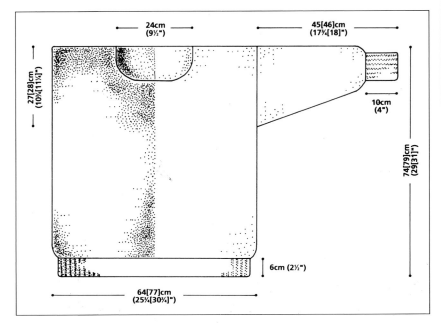

27[28]cm
(10¾[11¼]")

24cm
(9½")

45[46]cm
(17¾[18]")

10cm
(4")

74[79]cm
(29[31]")

6cm (2½")

64[77]cm
(25¾[30¾]")

*If I don't get that job as a
Bond girl after this . . .*

turn leaving rem sts on a spare needle.

Using A and working on first side of neck only, cast (bind) off 2 sts at beg of next row and every foll alt row 5 times in all, then dec one st at neck edge on 3 foll alt rows. 38[50] sts.

Work without shaping until there are same number of rows as Back to shoulder, ending with a WS row.

Cast (bind) off.

Return to rem sts and with RS facing, slip centre 20 sts onto a st holder, rejoin yarn B and K to end of row.

Work one row without shaping.

Cast (bind) off 2 sts at beg of next row and every foll alt row 5 times in all, then dec one st at neck edge on 3 foll alt rows.

38[50] sts.

Work without shaping until there are same number of rows as Back to shoulder, ending with a RS row.

Cast (bind) off.

SLEEVES

Using smaller needles and yarn A, cast on 44[50] sts.

Work 10cm (4") in K1, P1 rib, ending with a WS row.

Change to larger needles and beg with a K row, work in st st, inc one st at each end of next row and every foll alt row until there are 102[108] sts.

Cont in st st without shaping until Sleeve measures 45[46]cm (17¾[18]") from beg or desired length, ending with a WS row.

Cast (bind) off all sts.

Using yarn B only, make the 2nd Sleeve in the same way as the first.

CREWNECK NECKBAND

Press pieces on WS with a warm iron over a damp cloth, omitting ribbing.

Join right shoulder seam.

Using smaller needles and yarn A, pick up and K22 sts down left front neck, K10 sts from st holder, change to yarn B and pick up and K the foll 10 sts from st holder, pick up and K22 sts up right front neck and K23 sts from back neck st holder, change to a 2nd ball of yarn A and pick up and K the foll 23 sts from the st holder. 110 sts.**

Changing colour at centre front and centre back as set and working A sts in A and B sts in B, work 5cm (2") in K1, P1 rib.

Cast (bind) off in rib.

TURTLENECK COLLAR

Work as for crewneck neckband to **.

Changing colour at centre front and centre back as set and working A sts in A and B sts in B, work 4cm (1½") in K1, P1 rib, twisting yarn tog on WS of work when changing colour.

Twisting yarn tog on RS of sweater, cont in rib as set until ribbing measures 10cm (4") from beg.

Change to larger needles and cont as set until ribbing measures 20cm (8") from beg.

Cast (bind) off in rib.

FINISHING

Join left shoulder seam and neckband or collar.

Placing centre of cast (bound) off sleeve edge at shoulder seam, sew Sleeves to Back and Front, matching sides.

Join side and sleeve seams.

Press seams lightly on WS with a warm iron over a damp cloth, omitting ribbing.

PEACOCK LACE

SIZE
One size only (see page 107 for choosing size)
Finished measurement around bust 156cm (62")
See diagram for finished measurements of back, front and sleeves. To lengthen or shorten back and front, or sleeves see page 107.

MATERIALS
23 x 50g (1¾oz) balls of Rowan *Handknit DK Cotton* in either Peacock (shade no. 259) or Bathstone (shade no. 257)
One pair each 3¼mm (US size 3) and 4mm (US size 6) needles *or size to obtain correct tension (gauge)*

TENSION (GAUGE)
20 sts and 28 rows to 10cm (4") over st st on 4mm (US size 6) needles
Check your tension (gauge) before beginning

BACK
Using smaller needles, cast on 155 sts.
***Beg with a P row, work 5 rows in st st for hem, so ending with a P row.
Then work eyelet row (for hem foldline) as foll:
Eyelet row (RS) K2, *K2tog, take yarn to front between two needles, then take yarn from front to back over top of RH needle to make a new loop — called *yarn over* or *yo* —, rep from * to last st, K1.
Purl each st in next row (including each yo).
Beg with a K row, work 5 rows in st st, so ending with a K row.***
Change to larger needles and beg lace patt (worked over a multiple of 31 sts) as foll:
1st patt row (WS) Purl.
2nd row (RS) *K13, K2tog, yo, K1 tbl, yo, sl next 2 sts knitwise (one at a time) onto RH needle, insert tip of LH needle into fronts of 2 slipped sts and knit them tog

Has she got a headache? Or what?

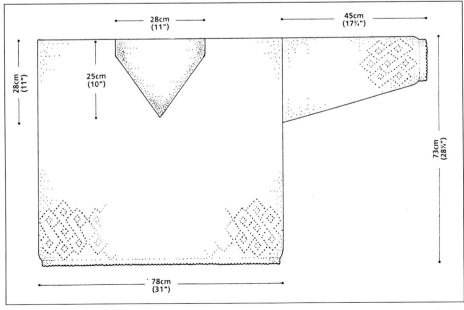

— called *slip, slip, knit* or *ssk* —, K13, rep from * to end (there are 5 patt reps across row on Back).
3rd row and all foll WS rows Purl each st (including each yo).
4th row *K12, K2tog, yo, K1 tbl, K1, K1 tbl, yo, ssk, K12, rep from * to end.
6th row *K11, K2tog, yo, K1 tbl, K3, K1 tbl, yo, ssk, K11, rep from * to end.
8th row *K10, K2tog, yo, K1 tbl, K1, K2tog, yo, K2, K1 tbl, yo, ssk, K10, rep from * to end.
10th row *K5, K2tog, yo, K1 tbl, yo, sl 1-K2tog-psso, yo, K1 tbl, K1, K2tog, yo, K1 tbl, yo, ssk, K1, K1 tbl, yo, K3tog, yo, K1 tbl, yo, ssk, K5, rep from * to end.
12th row *K4, (K2tog, yo, K1 tbl, K1, K1 tbl, yo, ssk, K1) 3 times, K3, rep from * to end.
14th row *K3, **K2tog, yo, K1 tbl, K3, K1 tbl, yo, ssk**, K1, K1 tbl, yo, sl 1-K2tog-psso, yo, K1 tbl, K1, rep from ** to ** once, K3, rep from * to end.
16th row *K2, **K2tog, yo, K1 tbl, K1, K2tog, yo, K2, K1 tbl, yo, ssk**, K1, K1 tbl, yo, ssk, K1, rep from ** to ** once, K2, rep from * to end.
18th row *K1, K2tog, **yo, K1 tbl, K1, K2 tog, yo, (K1 tbl, yo, ssk, K1) twice**, K1 tbl, yo, sl 1-K2tog-psso, rep from ** to ** once, rep from * to end.
20th row *K2tog, yo, K1 tbl, **K1, K2tog, yo, K1 tbl, K1, K1 tbl, yo, ssk, K1, K1 tbl, yo, ssk**, K1, K1 tbl, yo, ssk, rep from ** to ** once, rep from * to end.
22nd row *Work **K1, K1 tbl, yo, ssk, K1, K1 tbl, yo, sl 1-K2tog-psso, yo, K1 tbl, K1, K2tog, yo, K1 tbl**, yo, ssk, rep from ** to ** once, K1, rep from * to end.
24th row *K2, (K1 tbl, yo, ssk, K1) twice, **K2tog, yo, K1 tbl, K1**, (K1 tbl, yo, ssk, K1) 3 times, rep from ** to ** once, K1, rep from * to end.
26th row *K3, **K1 tbl, yo, ssk, K1, K1 tbl, yo, sl 1-K2tog-psso, yo, K1 tbl**, K1, K2tog, yo, K1

tbl, yo, ssk, K1, rep from ** to ** once, K3, rep from * to end.
28th row *K4, (K1 tbl, yo, ssk, K1) twice, K2tog, yo, K1 tbl, K1, (K1 tbl, yo, ssk, K1) 3 times, K3, rep from * to end.
30th row *K3, **K2tog, yo, K1 tbl, yo, ssk, K1, K1 tbl, yo, ssk**, K1, K1 tbl, yo, sl 1-K2tog-psso, yo, K1 tbl, K1, rep from ** to ** once, K3, rep from * to end.
32nd row *K2, **K2tog, yo, K1 tbl, K1**, (K1 tbl, yo, ssk, K1) 3 times, rep from ** to ** once, (K1 tbl, yo, ssk, K1) twice, K1, rep from * to end.
34th, 36th, 38th and 40th rows Rep 18th, 20th, 22nd and 24th rows.
42nd row *K3, **K1 tbl, yo, ssk, K1, K1 tbl, K1, K2tog, yo, K1 tbl**, K1`, K2tog, yo, K1 tbl, yo, ssk, K1, rep from ** to ** once, K3, rep from * to end.
44th row *K4, **K1 tbl, yo, ssk, K1, K2tog, yo, K1 tbl**, K1, K2tog, yo, K1 tbl, K1, K1 tbl, yo, ssk, K1, rep from ** to ** once, K4, rep from * to end.
46th row *K5, **K1 tbl, yo, sl 1-K2tog-psso, yo, K1 tbl**, yo, ssk, K1, rep from ** to ** once, K1, K2tog, yo, rep from ** to ** once, K5, rep from * to end.
48th row *K6, (K1 tbl, K1) twice, (K1 tbl, yo, ssk, K1) twice, K2tog, yo, (K1 tbl, K1) twice, K1 tbl, K6, rep from * to end.
50th row *K11, K1 tbl, yo, ssk, K1, K1 tbl, K1, K2tog, yo, K1 tbl, K11, rep from * to end.
52th row *K12, K1 tbl, yo, ssk, K1, K2tog, yo, K1 tbl, K12 , rep from * to end.
54th row *K13, K1 tbl, yo, sl 1-K2tog-psso, yo, K1 tbl, K13, rep from * to end.
56th row *K14, K1 tbl, K1, K1 tbl, K14, rep from * to end.
This completes lace insertion pattern.****
Beg with a P row, work in st st until Back measures 73cm (28¾") from hemline (eyelet row) or desired length, ending with a WS row.

A nifty top for those of us blessed in the bosom department. Great colour too.

Cast (bind) off 50 sts at beg of next 2 rows.
Slip rem 55 sts onto a st holder for back neck.

FRONT
Work as for Back to ****.
Beg with a P row, work in st st until Front measures 48cm (18¾") from hemline (eyelet row) or 25cm (10") less than desired length, ending with a WS row.

Shape V-neck
Cont in st st throughout, beg neck shaping on next row as foll:
Next row (RS) K75, K2tog, turn leaving rem sts on a spare needle. Working on first side of neck only, P one row, then dec one st end of next row (neck edge) and at end of every foll alt row until 50 sts rem.
Work without shaping until Front has same number of rows as Back, ending with a WS row.
Cast (bind) off.
Return to rem sts and with RS facing, slip centre st onto a safety pin, rejoin yarn to rem sts and K2tog, then K to end of row. P one row, then dec one st beg of next row (neck edge) and at beg of every foll alt row until 50 sts rem.
Work without shaping until Front has same number of rows as Back, ending with a RS row.
Cast (bind) off.

SLEEVES
Using smaller needles, cast on 51 sts.
Work picot hem as for Back from *** to ***, but increasing 11 sts evenly across last row of st st, so ending with a K row. 62 sts.
Change to larger needles and beg lace patt as foll:
1st patt row (WS) Purl.
2nd row (RS) K into front and back of first st, K12, *K2tog, yo, K1 tbl, yo, ssk*, K26, rep from * to * once, K12, K into front and back of last st. 64 sts.
3rd row Purl each st (including each yo).

4th row K into front and back of first st, slip a st marker onto RH needle; *K12, K2tog, yo, K1 tbl, K1, K1 tbl, yo, ssk, K12*, rep from * to * once; slip a st marker onto RH needle, K into front and back of last st. 66 sts.
5th row Keeping markers in place by slipping them from LH to RH needle when reached, purl to end.
6th row K into front and back of first st, K1, slip marker; *K11, K2tog, yo, K1 tbl, K3, K1 tbl, yo, ssk, K11*, rep from * to * once; slip marker, K1, K into front and back of next st. 68 sts.
7th row and all foll WS rows
Work as for 5th row.
Cont in this way foll lace patt as for Back from 8th row by working lace patt between markers *and at the same time* cont shaping Sleeve as before by inc one st at each end of every alt row (and working all extra sts outside markers in st st) until 48th lace patt row has been completed. 110 sts.
Without shaping, work in patt as set until 56th lace patt row has been completed.
Then work in st st only, until Sleeve measures 45cm (17¾") from hemline or desired length, ending with a WS row.
Cast (bind) off all sts.
Make 2nd Sleeve in the same way as the first.

NECKBAND
Press pieces lightly on WS with a warm iron over a damp cloth.
Join right shoulder seam.
Using smaller needles and with RS facing, pick up and K66 sts down left front neck, K centre st from safety pin, pick up and K66 sts up left front neck and K55 sts from back neck holder. 188 sts.
P one row.
Work eyelet row as foll:
Eyelet row (RS) K2tog, (yo, K2tog) 32 times, K centre st, *K2tog, yo, rep from * to the last st, K1.

Next row P to centre 3 sts on Front, P3tog, P to end.
K one row.
Next row P to centre 3 sts on Front, P3tog, P to end.
Cast (bind) off.

FINISHING
Join left shoulder seam and neckband.
Placing centre of cast (bound) off sleeve edge at shoulder seam, sew Sleeves to Back and Front, matching sides.
Join side and sleeve seams.
Turn under hem on Back and Front and Sleeves, folding along eyelet row, and sew lightly to WS. Turn under neckband and sew in place in same way.
Press seams lightly on WS with a warm iron over a damp cloth.

PASTEL ROSES

SIZE

One size only (see page 107 for choosing size)
Finished measurement around bust 136cm (54")
See diagram for finished measurements of back, front and sleeves. To lengthen or shorten back and front, or sleeves see page 107.

MATERIALS

Patons *Classic Cotton DK*
11 x 50g (1¾oz) balls in main colour — Almond (shade no. 2222) A
3 x 50g (1¾oz) balls in Pastel Yellow (shade no. 2227) B
2 x 50g (1¾oz) balls in Soft Amber (shade no. 2226) C
1 x 50g (1¾oz) ball each in Crystal Mint (shade no. 2244) D, Coral (shade no. 2224) E and Silver (shade no. 2228) F
One pair each 3¼mm (US size 3) and 4mm (US size 6) needles *or size to obtain correct tension (gauge)*
4.00mm (US size F/5) crochet hook

TENSION (GAUGE)

22 sts and 30 rows to 10cm (4") over st st on 4mm (US size 6) needles
Check your tension (gauge) before beginning.

NOTES

When working charted yoke patt, do not strand yarn across back of work, but use a separate ball or length of yarn for each isolated area of colour, twisting yarns at back when changing colours to avoid holes. Read chart from right to left for RS rows and from left to right for WS rows.

BACK

Using smaller needles and yarn B, cast on 149 sts. Break off yarn B. Using yarn A, beg K1, P1 rib as foll:
1st rib row (RS) P1, *K1, P1, rep from * to end.

2nd rib row K1, *P1, K1, rep from * to end.
Rep last 2 rows until ribbing measures 8cm (3¼") from beg, ending with a WS row.**
Change to larger needles and beg with a K row, work in st st until Back measures 44cm (17¼") from beg, ending with a WS row. Beg charted colour patt (see *Notes* above) on next row as foll:
1st chart row (RS) Using yarn A, K74, then change to yarn B and K1, using a separate ball of yarn A, K74.
2nd chart row P73 with yarn A, P3 with yarn B, P73 with yarn A.
Beg with 3rd chart row (K row), cont in st st foll chart for Back Yoke (page 38) until 90th chart row has been completed, so ending with a WS row.
Using yarn B only and cont in st st, cast (bind) off 51 sts at beg of next 2 rows.
Cast (bind) off rem 47 sts for back neck.

FRONT

Work as for Back to **.
Change to larger needles and beg with a K row, work in st st until there are same number of

rows as Back to beg of colour patt, ending with a WS row.
Beg with first chart row (K row), cont in st st foll chart for Back Yoke until 20th chart row has been completed, so ending with a WS row.

Shape V-neck

Cont to foll chart for colour patt and working in st st throughout, beg neck shaping on next row as foll:
21st chart row (RS) Work first 74 sts in patt, turn leaving rem sts on a spare needle.
Working on first side of neck only, dec one st at beg of next row (neck edge) and at neck edge on every foll alt row until 51 sts rem.
Work without shaping until 90th chart row has been completed.
Cast (bind) off.
Return to rem sts and with RS facing, rejoin yarn, cast (bind) off centre st, then work in patt to end of row.
Dec one st at end of next row (neck edge) and at neck edge on every foll alt row until 51 sts rem.
Work without shaping until 91st chart row has been completed.
Cast (bind) off.

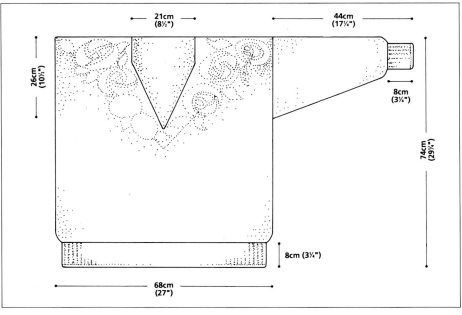

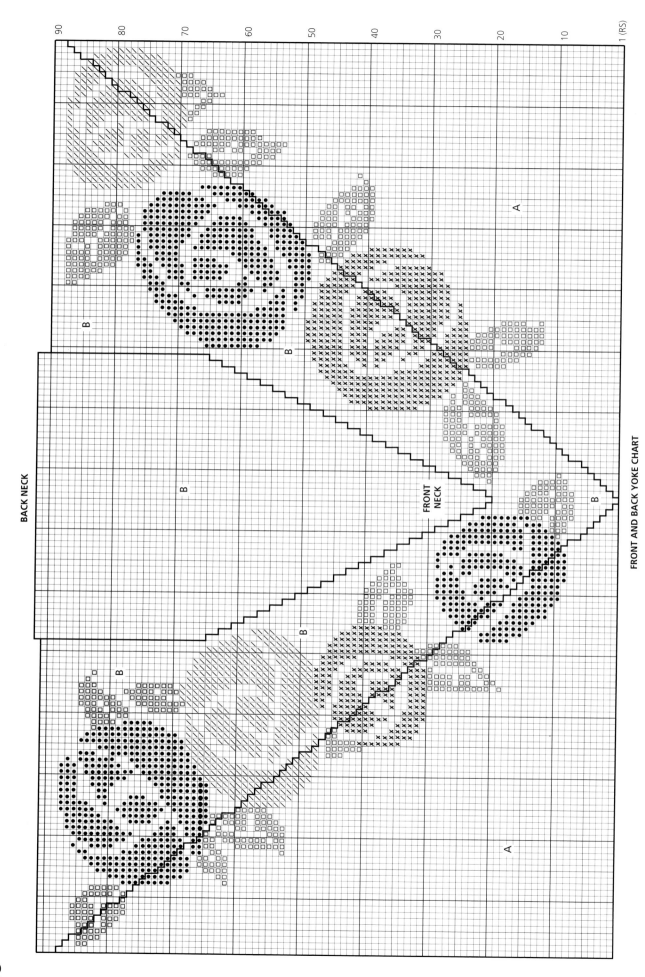

BACK NECK

FRONT NECK

FRONT AND BACK YOKE CHART

SLEEVES

Using smaller needles and yarn B, cast on 51 sts. Break off yarn B. Using yarn A, work 8cm (3¼") in K1, P1 rib as for Back, ending with a WS row.

Change to larger needles and beg with a K row, work in st st, inc one st at each end of 3rd row and then every foll alt row until there are 115 sts, so ending with a RS row.

Work in st st without shaping until Sleeve measures 44cm (17¼") from beg or desired length, ending with a WS row. Cast (bind) off all sts.

Make the 2nd Sleeve in the same way as the first.

PICOT NECK EDGING

Press pieces lightly on WS with a warm iron over a damp cloth, omitting ribbing.

Join shoulder seams.

Using crochet hook and yarn B and with RS facing, beg at right shoulder seam work evenly along neck edge as foll:

Edging round (RS) *Work 3dc (US single crochet or *3sc*) evenly spaced along edge, 2ch, 1dc (*1sc*) into top of last dc (*sc*) to form a picot*, rep from * to * all along back neck, down left front neck and up right front neck, joining with a slip st into first st of round. Fasten off.

FINISHING

Placing centre of cast (bound) off sleeve edge at shoulder seam, sew Sleeves to Back and Front, matching sides.

Join side and sleeve seams.

Press seams lightly on WS with a warm iron over a damp cloth, omitting ribbing.

COLOUR KEY

☐ = A (Almond) — outside outer 'V'
☐ = B (Pastel yellow) — inside outer and inner 'V'
⊡ = C (Soft Amber)
☑ = D (Crystal Mint)
☒ = E (Coral)
⊡ = F (Silver)

Soooo girlie . . .

CABLE MOSS

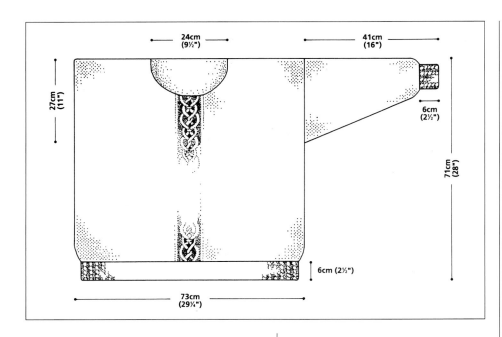

24cm (9½") — **41cm (16")** — **27cm (11")** — **6cm (2½")** — **71cm (28")** — **6cm (2½")** — **73cm (29¼")**

SIZE
One size only (see page 107 for choosing size)
Finished measurement around bust 146cm (58½")
See diagram for finished measurements of back, front and sleeves. To lengthen or shorten back and front, or sleeves see page 107.

MATERIALS
20 x 50g (1¾oz) balls of Jaeger *Pure Cotton Double Knitting* in Ecru (shade no. 605)
One pair each 3¼mm (US size 3) and 4mm (US size 6) needles *or size to obtain correct tension (gauge)*
Cable needle (cn)
2 stitch markers (see *Notes*)

TENSION (GAUGE)
21 sts and 38 rows to 10cm (4") over moss (seed) st on 4mm (US size 6) needles
Check your tension (gauge) before beginning.

NOTES
A cable panel is worked up the Front. Instructions are given for placing st markers on either side of the panel. These st markers are slipped in each row so that they are always positioned on the needles on either side of the panel as a guide for the knitter. An experienced knitter may not find the st markers necessary.

MOSS (SEED) STITCH
The foll instructions are for working moss (seed) st over an even number of sts.
1st row (WS) *K1, P1, rep from * to end.
2nd row *P1, K1, rep from * to end.
The last 2 rows are repeated to form the moss (seed) st patt over an even number of sts.

CABLE PANEL
This panel is worked over 26 sts and is begun on a WS row.
1st row (WS) P3, K4, (P4, K4) twice, P3.
2nd row (RS) P2, sl 1 (slip 3rd and 3rd to last sts of panel on RS rows purlwise and with yarn at back of work), P4, slip next 2 sts onto a cable needle (cn) and hold at back of work, K next 2 sts from LH needle, then K2 from cn — called *cable 4 back* or *C4B —*,

P4, slip next 2 sts onto a cn and hold at front of work, K next 2 sts from LH needle, then K2 from cn — called *cable 4 front* or *C4F —*, P4, sl 1, P2.
3rd row As first row.
4th row P2, sl 1, P3, slip next st onto a cn and hold at back of work, K next 2 sts from LH needle, then P1 from cn — called *twist 3 back* or *T3B —*, slip next 2 sts onto a cn and hold at front of work, P next st from LH needle, then K2 from cn — called *twist 3 front* or *T3F —*, P2, T3B, T3F, P3, sl 1, P2.
5th row P3, K3, P2, (K2, P2) 3 times, K3, P3.
6th row P2, sl 1, P2, (T3B, P2, T3F) twice, P2, sl 1, P2.
7th row P3, K2, P2, K4, P4, K4, P2, K2, P3.
8th row P2, sl 1, P2, K2, P4, C4B, P4, K2, P2, sl 1, P2.
9th row As 7th row.
10th row P2, sl 1, P2, K2, P4, K4, P4, K2, P2, sl 1, P2.
11th and 12th rows As 7th and 8th rows.
13th row As 7th row.
14th row P2, sl 1, P2, (T3F, P2, T3B) twice, P2, sl 1, P2.
15th row As 5th row.
16th row P2, sl 1, P3, T3F, T3B, P2, T3F, T3B, P3, sl 1, P2.
17th and 18th rows As first and 2nd rows.
19th row As first row.
20th and 21st rows As 4th and 5th rows.
22nd row P2, sl 1, P3, K2, P2, then work K2, P2, K2 over next 6 sts and slip these 6 sts onto a cn, wrap yarn anticlockwise (counterclockwise) 4 times around these 6 sts, then slip them back onto RH needle — called *cluster 6 —*, P2, K2, P3, sl 1, P2.
23rd row As 5th row.
24th row As 16th row.
These 24 rows are repeated to form the cable patt.

This shot is really not of the fab jumper but a chance for the orally curious to count my teeth . . .

BACK

Using smaller needles, cast on 154 sts.
Beg cable rib as foll:
1st rib row (RS) P1, *K2, P1, rep from * to end.
2nd rib row K1, *P2, K1, rep from * to end.
3rd rib row P1, *take RH needle behind first st on LH needle and K the 2nd st tbl, then K first st and slip both sts tog off LH needle, P1, rep from * to end.
4th rib row As 2nd row.
Rep last 4 rows until cable ribbing measures 6cm (2½") from beg, ending with a first (RS) row.**
Change to larger needles and work in moss (seed) st until Back measures 71cm (28") from beg, ending with a WS row.
Cast (bind) off 52 sts at beg of next 2 rows.
Slip rem 50 sts onto a st holder for back neck.

FRONT

Work as for Back to **..
Change to larger needles and position patt sts across Front (see *Notes* above) as foll:
1st patt row (WS) Work first row of moss (seed) st over first 64 sts and slip st marker onto RH needle; work first row of cable panel over next 26 sts and slip on st marker; work first row of moss (seed) st over last 64 sts.
2nd patt row Work 2nd row of moss (seed) st over first 64 sts and slip marker; work 2nd row of cable panel over next 26 sts and slip marker; work 2nd row of moss (seed) st over last 64 sts.
Cont in patt as set (working cable panel between markers and foll row by row instructions for st patts) until there are 34 rows less than Back to shoulder and Front measures approx 61cm (24") from beg, ending with a WS row.
Shape Neck
Keeping patt correct throughout, beg neck shaping on next row as foll:
Next row (RS) Work 72 sts in patt, turn leaving rem sts on a spare needle.
Working on first side of neck only, dec one st at neck edge on next 20 rows. 52 sts.
Work without shaping until there are same number of rows as Back to shoulder, ending with a WS row.
Cast (bind) off.
Return to rem sts and with RS facing, slip centre 10 sts onto a st holder, then rejoin yarn and work in patt to end of row.
Dec one st at neck edge on next 20 rows. 52 sts.
Work without shaping until there are same number of rows as Back to shoulder, ending with a RS row.
Cast (bind) off.

SLEEVES

Using smaller needles, cast on 49 sts.
Work 6cm (2½") in cable rib as for Back, ending with a 4th (WS) row.
Inc 23 sts evenly across next row as foll:
Inc row (RS) Rib 2, (insert LH needle from front to back under horizontal strand between st just worked and next st and K through back of this st to twist it — called *make one* or *M1* —, rib 2) 22 times, M1, rib 3. 72 sts.
Change to larger needles and work in moss (seed) st, inc one st at each end of 3rd and every foll alt row until there are 116 sts, keeping moss (seed) st patt correct.
Work in moss (seed) st without shaping until Sleeve measures 41cm (16") from beg or desired length, ending with a WS row.
Cast (bind) off all sts in patt.
Make the 2nd Sleeve in the same way as the first.

COLLAR

Do not press.
Join right shoulder seam.
Using smaller needles and with RS facing, pick up and K27 down left front neck, K10 sts from front neck st holder, pick up and K28 sts up right front neck and K50 sts from back neck st holder. 115 sts.
Beg rib as foll:
1st rib row (P1, K2) 27 times, P4, *K2, P1, rep from * to end.
2nd rib row (K1, P2) 10 times, K4, *P2, K1, rep from * to end.
Rep last 2 rows twice more.
Divide Collar
Next row (RS) P1, (take RH needle behind first st on LH needle and K the 2nd st tbl, then K first st and slip both sts tog off LH needle, P1) 27 times, turn leaving rem 33 sts on a st holder. 82 sts.
***Beg with a 4th rib row as for Back, cont in cable rib until Collar measures 9cm (3½").
Cast (bind) off evenly in rib.***
Return to rem sts and with RS facing and beg at centre front neck, rejoin yarn, cast (bind) off 2 sts purlwise (one st now already on RH needle), then across rem 30 sts work — (take RH needle behind first st on LH needle and K the 2nd st tbl, then K first st and slip both sts tog off LH needle, P1) 10 times.
Complete as for first side of Collar from *** to ***.

FINISHING

Join left shoulder seam and collar.
Placing centre of cast (bound) off sleeve edge at shoulder seam, sew Sleeves to Back and Fronts, matching sides.
Join side and sleeve seams.
Press seams lightly on WS with a warm iron over a damp cloth, omitting ribbing.

SAILOR STRIPES

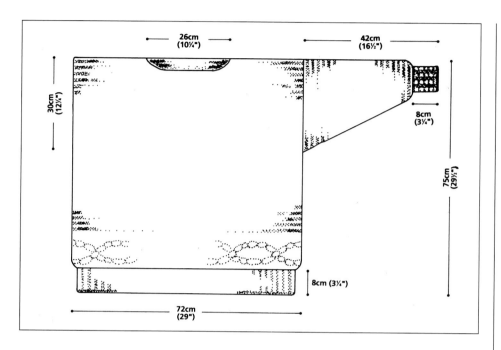

SIZE
One size only (see page 107 for choosing size)
Finished measurement around bust 144cm (58")
See diagram for finished measurements of back, front and sleeves. To lengthen or shorten back and front, or sleeves see page 107.

MATERIALS
Twilleys *Pegasus*
6 x 100g (3½oz) hanks in Blue (shade no. 86) A
7 x 100g (3½oz) hanks Ecru (shade no. 2) B
One pair each 4mm (US size 6) and 4½mm (US size 7) needles *or size to obtain correct tension (gauge)*

TENSION (GAUGE)
18 sts and 24 rows to 10cm (4") over st st on 4½mm (US size 7) needles
Check your tension (gauge) before beginning.

NOTES
When working chain border along lower back and front,
strand yarns A and B loosely across back of work only along chain link shapes. Do not strand yarns across large oval shapes (in ecru) at centre of 'chains', but use a separate length of yarn for each isolated area of colour, twisting yarns at back when changing colours to avoid holes. Read chart from right to left for RS (knit) rows and from left to right for WS (purl) rows.*

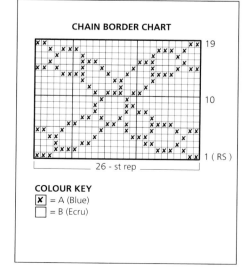

CHAIN BORDER CHART

19

10

1 (RS)

26 - st rep

COLOUR KEY
☒ = A (Blue)
☐ = B (Ecru)

BACK
Using smaller needles and yarn A, cast on 130 sts. Break off yarn A. Change to yarn B and beg K2, P2 rib as foll:
1st rib row (RS) P2, *K2, P2, rep from * to end.
2nd rib row K2, *P2, K2, rep from * to end.
Rep last 2 rows until ribbing measures 8cm (3¼") from beg, ending with a WS row.
Change to larger needles and beg with a K row, work 2 rows in st st, so ending with a WS row. Cont in st st throughout and beg with first chart row, foll chart for chain border (see *Notes* above), working 26-st rep 5 times across the row, until 19th chart row has been completed, so ending with a RS (knit) row.
Using yarn B only and beg with a P row, work 7 rows in st st, so ending with a WS row.
Cont in st st throughout, beg stripe patt as foll:
Work 2 rows in yarn A and 2 rows in yarn B.**
Rep from ** to ** until Back measures 75cm (29½") from beg, ending with a WS row.
Keeping to patt as set, cast (bind) off 42 sts at beg of next 2 rows.
Slip rem 46 sts onto a st holder for back neck.

FRONT
Work as for Back until there are 10 rows less than Back to beg of shoulder shaping, so ending with a WS row.
Shape Neck
Keeping to patt as set, beg neck shaping on next row as foll:
Next row (RS) K50, K2tog, turn leaving rem sts on spare a needle. Working on first side of neck only, dec one st at neck edge on every row 9 times. 42 sts.
Cast (bind) off.
Return to rem st and with RS facing, slip centre 26 sts onto a st holder, rejoin yarn, K2tog, then K to end of row.
Complete 2nd side of neck to

I'd use the word nautical – what do you think?

match first side, reversing all shaping.

SLEEVES

Using smaller needles and yarn A, cast on 42 sts. Do not break off yarn A.
Change to yarn B and work 2 rows in K2, P2 rib as for Back, then cont in rib as set, change to yarn A and work 2 rows.
Rep last 4 rows until ribbing measures 8cm (3¼") from beg, ending with a WS row.
Change to larger needles and cont in stripe patt of 2 rows A and 2 rows B, beg with a K row and work in stripe patt in st st throughout *and at the same time* inc one st at each end of 3rd row and then every foll alt row until there are 110 sts.
Work without shaping until Sleeve measures 42cm (16½") from beg or desired length, ending with a WS row.
Cast (bind) off all sts.
Make the 2nd Sleeve in the same way as the first.

COLLAR

Press pieces lightly on WS with a warm iron over a damp cloth, omitting ribbing.
Join right shoulder seam.
Using smaller needles and yarn A and with RS facing, pick up and K8 sts down left front neck, then across 26 sts of front neck st holder work — (K2, K into front and back of next st) 8 times, K2, pick up and K8 sts up right front neck, then across 46 sts of back neck st holder work — K into front and back of first st, (K2, K into front and back of next st) 15 times. 112 sts.
Work 28cm (11") in K2, P2 rib.
Cast (bind) off loosely in rib.

FINISHING

Join left shoulder seam and collar.
Placing centre of cast (bound) off sleeve edge at shoulder seam, sew Sleeves to Back and Front, matching sides.
Join side and sleeve seams.
Press seams lightly on WS with a warm iron over a damp cloth, omitting ribbing.

SUMMER SHIRT

SIZE
One size only (see page 107 for choosing size)
Finished measurement around bust 140cm (55")
See diagram for finished measurements of back, front and sleeves. To lengthen or shorten back and front, or sleeves see page 107.

MATERIALS
18 x 50g (1¾oz) balls of Jaeger *Pure Cotton* in Ecru (shade no. 605)
One pair each 3¼mm (US size 3) and 4mm (US size 6) needles *or size to obtain correct tension (gauge)*
Three 1.5cm (⅝") buttons

TENSION (GAUGE)
22 sts and 30 rows to 10cm (4") over st st on 4mm (US size 6) needles
32 sts (2 patt reps) to 14cm (5½in) and 30 rows (3 patt reps) to 10cm (4") over 'closed' patt st on 4mm (US size 6) needles
Check your tension (gauge) before beginning.

BACK
Using smaller needles, cast on 160 sts.
Work 4cm (1½") in garter st (K every row), ending with a WS row.
Change to larger needles and beg openwork patt st (worked over a multiple of 16 sts) as foll:
1st patt row (RS) Knit.
2nd patt row *K4, P8, K4, rep from * to end. (There are 10 patt reps across Back).
3rd patt row *P3, K2tog, K3, take yarn to front between two needles, then take yarn from front to back over top of RH needle and around to front again, take yarn from front to back again over top of RH needle to make 2 new loops — called *double yarn over* or *yo2* —, K3, sl next 2 sts knitwise (one at a time) onto RH needle, insert tip of LH

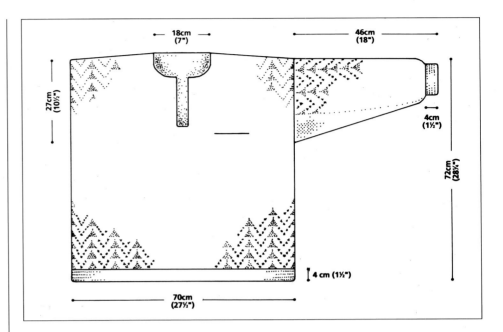

needle into fronts of 2 slipped sts and knit them tog — called *slip, slip, knit* or *ssk* —, P3, rep from * to end.

4th patt row *K3, P4, purl into front of first yo and back of 2nd yo, P4, K3, rep from * to end.

5th patt row *P2, K2tog, K3, take yarn to front between two needles, then take yarn from front to back over top of RH needle to make a new loop — called *yarn over* or *yo* —, K2, yo, K3, ssk, P2, rep from * to end.

6th patt row *K2, P12, K2, rep from * to end.

7th patt row *P1, K2tog, K3, yo, K4, yo, K3, ssk, P1, rep from * to end.

8th patt row *K1, P14, K1, rep from * to end.

9th patt row *K2tog, K3, yo, K6, yo, K3, ssk, rep from * to end.

10th patt row Purl.

Rep first-10th patt rows 6 times more.

Then beg 'closed' patt st as foll:

1st row (RS) Knit.

2nd row *K4, P8, K4, rep from * to end.

3rd row *P3, K2tog, K3, insert LH needle from front to back under horizontal strand between last st worked and next st on LH needle, then knit into first the back and then the front of this st — called *make 2* or *M2* —, K3, ssk, P3, rep from * to end.

4th row *K3, P10, K3, rep from * to end.

5th row *P2, K2tog, K3, insert LH needle from front to back under horizontal strand between last st worked and next st on LH needle, then knit into the back of this st — called *make one* or *M1* —, K2, M1, K3, ssk, P2, rep from * to end.

6th row *K2, P12, K2, rep from * to end.

7th row *P1, K2tog, K3, M1, K4, M1, K3, ssk, P1, rep from * to end.

8th row *K1, P14, K1, rep from * to end.

9th row *K2tog, K3, M1, K6, M1, K3, ssk, rep from * to end.
10th row Purl.**
Rep last 10 rows 11 times more, so ending with a 10th patt row. Back measures approx 72cm (28¼") from beg.
Shape Shoulders
Next row Cast (bind) off 30 sts, K to end. 130 sts.
Next row Cast (bind) off 30 sts (one st already on RH needle), K5, *P8, K8, rep from *, ending last rep K6 instead of K8. 100 sts.
Next row Cast (bind) off 30 sts (one st already on RH needle), P6, *K2tog, K3, M2, K3, ssk, P6, rep from *, ending last rep P5 instead of P6.
Next row Cast (bind) off 30 sts (one st already on RH needle), *K6, P10, rep from *, ending last rep P1 instead of P10.
Cast (bind) off rem 40 sts for back neck.

FRONT
Before beg Front, make pocket lining.
Pocket Lining
Using larger needles, cast on 24 sts.
Work in st st until lining measures 11cm (4½in) from beg.
Break off yarn and slip sts onto a st holder to be used later when placing pocket.
Begin Front
Work as for Back to **.
Rep last 10 rows 4 times more, so ending with a 10th patt row.
Front measures approx 49cm (19") from beg.
Place Pocket
Cont in patt as set throughout, place pocket on next row (a first row) as foll:
Next row (RS) K34 sts, slip next 24 sts onto a st holder, then with RS of pocket lining facing, K the 24 sts of the pocket lining from the st holder, K to end.
Work 3 rows in patt, so ending with a 4th patt row. Front measures approx 50cm (19½") from beg.

Divide for Neck Opening
Divide for neck opening on next row (a 5th row) as foll:
5th row *P2, K2tog, K3, M1, K2, M1, K3, ssk, P2*, rep from * to * 3 times more, P2, K2tog, K3, M1, K5, turn leaving rem sts on a spare needle.
Working on first side of neck only, cont in patt as foll:
6th row P10, *K4, P12*, rep from * to * 3 times more, K2.
7th row *P1, K2tog, K3, M1, K4, M1, K3, ssk, P1*, rep from * to * 3 times more, P1, K2tog, K3, M1, K6.
8th row P11, *K2, P14*, rep from * to * 3 times more, K1.
9th row *K2tog, K3, M1, K6, M1, K3, ssk*, rep from * to * 3 times more, K2tog, K3, M1, K7.
10th row Purl.
Then beg from first patt row again as foll:
1st row Knit.
2nd row P8, *K8, P8*, rep from * to * 3 times more, K4.
3rd row *P3, K2tog, K3, M2, K3, ssk, P3*, rep from * to * 3 times more, P3, K2tog, K3, M1, K4.
4th row P9, *K6, P10*, rep from * to * 3 times more, K3.
5th row *P2, K2tog, K3, M1, K2, M1, K3, ssk, P2*, rep from * to * 3 times more, P2, K2tog, K3, M1, K5.
Cont in this way until 10 repeats of 'closed' patt st have been worked, but ending with a 9th patt row instead of a 10th patt row. Front measures approx 65cm (25¼") from beg.
Shape Neck
Keeping patt correct throughout, cast (bind) off 8 sts at beg of next row (neck edge), dec one st at neck edge on next 4 rows, then dec one st at neck edge on 4 foll alt rows, so ending with a 2nd patt row. 60 sts.
Without shaping, work 3rd to 10th patt rows, so ending with a WS row.
Front now measures same as Back to shoulder.

Shape Shoulder
Cast (bind) off 30 sts at beg of next and foll alt row.
Second Side of Neck
Return to rem sts and with RS facing, rejoin yarn and cast (bind) off centre 8 sts, then across rem 76 sts (a 5th patt row) beg working as foll:
5th row One st already on RH needle after centre cast (bind) off, K4, M1, K3, ssk, *P4, K2tog, K3, M1, K2, M1, K3, ssk*, rep from * to * 3 times more, P2.
6th row *K2, P12, K2*, rep from * to * 3 times more, K2, P10.
7th row K6, M1, K3, ssk, *P2, K2tog, K3, M1, K4, M1, K3, ssk*, rep from * to * 3 times more, P1.
8th row *K1, P14, K1*, rep from * to * 3 times more, K1, P11.
9th row K7, M1, K3, ssk, *K2tog, K3, M1, K6, M1, K3, ssk*, rep from * to * 3 times more.
10th row Purl.
Then beg from first patt row again as foll:
1st row Knit.
2nd row *K4, P8, K4*, rep from * to * 3 times more, K4, P8.
3rd row K4, M1, K3, ssk, *P6, K2tog, K3, M2, K3, ssk*, rep from * to * 3 times more, P3.
4th row *K3, P10, K3*, rep from * to * 3 times more, K3, P9.
Cont in this way until 10 repeats of 'closed' patt st have been worked, ending with a 10th patt row.
Work neck and shoulder shaping as for first side of neck, reversing all shaping.

SLEEVES
Using smaller needles, cast on 50 sts.
Work 4cm (1½") in garter st (K every row), ending with a RS row.
Inc 30 sts evenly across next row as foll:
Next row (inc row) K1, K into front and back of next st — called *inc 1* —, *K1, inc 1 in each of next 3 sts, (K1, inc 1) 3 times, rep from *, ending last rep (K1,

inc 1) twice instead of 3 times. 80 sts.
Change to larger needles and beg openwork patt st as foll:
1st patt row (RS) Knit.
2nd patt row *K4, P8, K4, rep from * to end.
(There are 5 patt reps across Sleeve.)
3rd patt row K into front and back of first st, P2, *K2tog, K3, yo2, K3, ssk, P6, rep from *, ending last rep P2, K into front and back of last st instead of P6. 82 sts.
4th patt row K4, *P4, purl into front of first yo and back of 2nd yo, P4, K6, rep from *, ending last rep K4 instead of K6.
5th patt row K1, *P2, K2tog, K3, yo, K2, yo, K3, ssk, P2, rep from * to last st, K1.
6th patt row K3, *P12, K4, rep from *, ending last rep K3 instead of K4.
7th patt row K into front and back of first st, slip a st marker onto RH needle; *P1, K2tog, K3, yo, K4, yo, K3, ssk, P1, rep from * to last st; slip a st marker onto RH needle, K into front and back of last st. 84 sts.
8th patt row P1, K1, slip marker; *K1, P14, K1, rep from * to marker; slip marker, P1, K1.
9th patt row K1, P1, slip marker; *K2tog, K3, yo, K6, yo, K3, ssk, rep from * to marker; slip marker, K1, P1.
10th patt row P1, K1, slip marker; purl to marker; P1, K1.
Cont in this way, working 5 patt reps (as for openwork patt on Back) between markers *and at the same time* inc one st at each end of next row and then every foll 4th row, working increased sts in moss (seed) st, until there are 118 sts.
Work in patt as set without shaping until the Sleeve measures 46cm (18") from beg or desired length, ending with a WS row.
Cast (bind) off loosely in patt.
Make the 2nd Sleeve in the same way as the first.

BUTTONHOLE BAND
Using smaller needles and with RS facing, pick up and K38 sts evenly up right front neck opening.
Work 5 rows in K1, P1 rib, so ending with a WS row.
Work buttonholes on next 2 rows as foll:
1st buttonhole row (RS) Rib 3, *cast (bind) off next 2 sts in rib, rib 13 counting st already on needle after cast (bind) off, rep from * once, cast (bind) off next 2 sts in rib, rib to end.
2nd buttonhole row (WS) Rib, casting on 2 sts over those cast (bound) off in last row.
Work 3 rows more in rib.
Cast (bind) off in rib.

BUTTON BAND
Using smaller needles and with RS facing, pick up and K38 sts evenly down left front neck opening.
Work 10 rows in K1, P1 rib.
Cast (bind) off in rib.

COLLAR
Using smaller needles, cast on 148 sts.
Work Collar in garter st as foll:
1st-3rd rows Knit.
4th row K4, K into front and back of next st, K to last 6 sts, K into front and back of next st, K5. 150 sts.
Rep last 4 rows 4 times more. 158 sts.
Work in garter st without shaping until Collar measures 10cm (4") from beg.
Cast (bind) off.

FINISHING
Press pieces lightly on WS with a warm iron over a damp cloth, omitting garter st and ribbing.
Pocket Top
Using smaller needles and with RS facing, K24 sts of pocket top from st holder. Work 4cm (1½") in garter st and cast (bind) off.
Sew pocket lining to WS of Front.
Sew ends of pocket top to RS.

With RS facing, place Buttonhole Band over Button Band. Sew row ends of Bands to 8 cast (bound) off sts at beg of neck opening.
Join shoulder seams.
Sew cast on edge of Collar to neck edge with ends halfway across front bands, making sure that seam does not show when Collar is turned down.
Placing centre of cast (bound) off sleeve edge at shoulder seam, sew Sleeves to Back and Front, matching sides.
Join side and sleeve seams.
Sew on buttons to correspond to buttonholes.
Press seams lightly on WS with a warm iron over a damp cloth, omitting garter st and ribbing.

LACE LOOK

SIZE
One size only (see page 107 for choosing size)
Finished measurement around bust 154cm (60½")
See diagram for finished measurements of back, front and sleeves. To lengthen or shorten back and front, or sleeves see page 107.

MATERIALS
15 x 50g (1¾oz) balls of Rowan *Handknit DK Cotton* Ecru (shade no. 251)
One pair each 5mm (US size 8) and 5½mm (US size 9) needles *or size to obtain correct tension (gauge)*

TENSION (GAUGE)
9 sts (one patt rep) to 7cm (2¾") and 16 rows (2 patt reps) to 8cm (3¼") over lace patt on 5½mm (US size 9) needles
Check your tension (gauge) before beginning.

NOTE
Lace patt is very stretchy, so when checking tension (gauge) lay swatch flat and smooth out, but do not pull excessively.

BACK
Using larger needles, cast on 99 sts.
Beg lace patt (worked over a multiple of 9 sts) as foll:
1st patt row (WS) Purl.
2nd patt row (RS) *K2, K2tog, take yarn to front between two needles, then take yarn from front to back over top of RH needle to make a new loop — called *yarn over* or *yo* —, K1, yo, sl next 2 sts knitwise (one at a time) onto RH needle, insert tip of LH needle into fronts of 2 slipped sts and knit them tog — called *slip, slip, knit* or *ssk* —, K2, rep from * to end (there are 11 patt reps across row on Back).
3rd patt row Purl each st (including each yo).
4th patt row *K1, K2tog, yo,

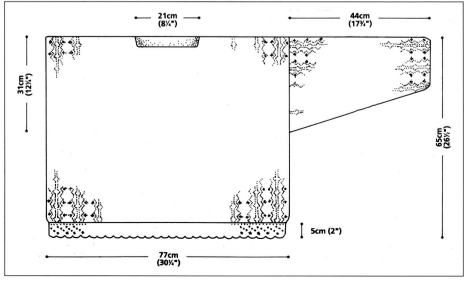

K3, yo, ssk, Kl, rep from * to end.
5th patt row Purl.
6th patt row *K1, yo, ssk, yo, slip 2 knitwise-K1-p2sso, yo, K2tog, yo, K1, rep from * to end.
7th patt row Purl.
8th patt row *K3, yo, sl 2 knitwise-K1-p2sso, yo, K3, rep from * to end.
First-8th patt rows form one patt rep.
Rep first-8th patt rows until 15 patt reps (120 rows) have been completed and Back measures approx 60cm (24½") from beg, so ending with an 8th patt row.
Cast (bind) off all sts in purl.

FRONT
Work as for Back until Front measures 8 rows (one patt rep) less than Back, so ending with an 8th patt row.

Shape Neck
Beg neck shaping on next row as foll:
Next row (WS) P36, turn leaving rem sts on a spare needle.
Working on first side of neck only, work 2nd-8th patt rows.
Cast (bind) off all sts in purl.
Return to rem sts and with WS facing, rejoin yarn, cast (bind) off centre 27 sts and P to end.
Complete 2nd side of neck to match first side.

SLEEVES
Using larger needles, cast on 45 sts.
Work first-8th patt rows as for Back *and at the same time*, keeping patt correct, inc one st at each end of 3rd row and then at each end of every foll alt row, until there are 81 sts (9 patt reps across row). *Note*: In order to keep patt correct, work increased sts at each end of row in st st until there are 9 extra sts, then beg working these 9 extra sts in patt.
Work in patt as set without shaping until 11 patt reps (88 rows) have been completed and Sleeve measures approx 44cm (17¾") from beg, so ending with a RS row.
Cast (bind) off all sts in purl.
Make the 2nd Sleeve in the same way as the first.

NECKBAND
Press pieces lightly on WS with a warm iron.
Join right shoulder seam, matching patt.
Using smaller needles and with RS facing, pick up and K6 sts down left front neck, 30 sts across centre front, 6 sts up left front neck and 31 sts across back neck. 73 sts.

Now with WS facing, cast (bind) off all sts in knit.

CUFFS
Join left shoulder seam and neckband.
Placing centre of cast (bound) off sleeve edge at shoulder seam, sew Sleeves to Back and Front, matching sides.
Using smaller needles and with RS facing, pick up and K45 sts across lower edge of sleeve (one st picked up in each cast-on st).
Now with WS facing, cast (bind) off all sts in knit.
Work 2nd cuff in same way.

LOWER BORDER
Join side and sleeve seams. Using larger needles, cast on 8 sts and K one row.
Then beg edging as foll:
1st row (WS) Sl 1, K1, insert LH needle from front to back under horizontal strand between last st worked and next st on LH needle, thus forming loop on LH needle, then K through front loop of this st — called *make one* or *M1* —, K2tog, M1, K2tog, K1, insert LH needle from front to back under horizontal strand between last st worked and next st on LH needle, then (K1, P1, K1) all through front loop of this st — called *make 3* or *M3* —, K1. (11 sts)
2nd row K2, P1, K8.
3rd row Sl 1, (K1, M1, K2tog) twice, K4.
4th row K11.
5th row Sl 1, K1, M1, K2tog, K2, M1, K2tog, K3.
6th row Cast (bind) off 3 sts, K to end. (8 sts)
Rep first-6th rows of border patt until edging fits all the way around the lower edge, ending with a 6th patt row.
Cast (bind) off.

FINISHING
Sew edging to lower edge and join edging seam.
Press seams lightly on WS with a warm iron.

Your grandad would've called it a string vest – we chose to think of it as modern and essentially feminine.

BOUCLE JACKET

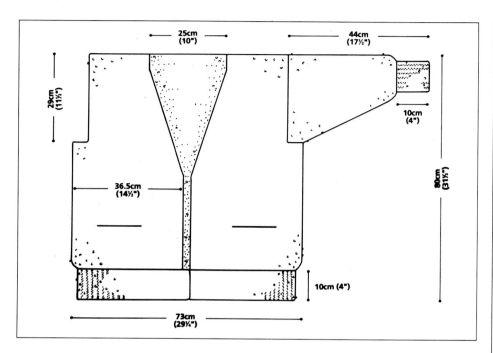

25cm (10")

44cm (17½")

29cm (11½")

36.5cm (14½")

10cm (4")

80cm (31½")

10cm (4")

73cm (29¼")

SIZE
One size only (see page 107 for choosing size)
Finished measurement around bust 149cm (59¼")
See diagram for finished measurements of back, fronts and sleeves. To lengthen o r shorten back and fronts, or sleeves see page 107.

MATERIALS
18 x 50g (1¾oz) balls of Wendy *Capri* in Rivulet (shade no. 118)
One pair each 3¼mm (US size 3) and 4½mm (US size 7) needles *or size to obtain correct tension (gauge)*

TENSION (GAUGE)
20 sts and 29 rows to 10cm (4") over st st on 4½mm (US size 7) needles
Check your tension (gauge) before beginning.

BACK
Using smaller needles, cast on 146 sts.
Beg K1, P1 rib as foll:
1st rib row (RS) *K1, P1, rep from * to last 2 sts, K2.

Rep last row until ribbing measures 10cm (4") from beg, ending with a WS row.
Change to larger needles and beg with a K row, work in st st until Back measures 51cm (20") from beg, ending with a WS row.
Shape Armholes
Cont in st st throughout, cast (bind) off 10 sts at beg of next 2 rows. 126 sts.
Work without shaping until Back measures 80cm (31½") from beg, ending with a WS row.
Cast (bind) off 38 sts at beg of next 2 rows. Cast (bind) off rem 50 sts for back neck.

LEFT FRONT
Before beg Left Front, make pocket lining.
Pocket Lining
Using larger needles, cast on 27 sts.
Work in st st until lining measures 14cm (5½") from beg, ending with a WS (P) row.
Break off yarn and slip sts onto a st holder to be used later.
Begin Left Front
Using smaller needles, cast on 82 sts for Left Front.

Work 10cm (4") in K1, P1 rib as for Back, ending with a WS row.****
Change to larger needles and work next row as foll:
Next row (RS) K73, turn leaving rem 9 sts on a st holder to be used later for front band.
Beg with a P row, cont in st st until Left Front measures 24cm (9½") from beg, ending with a WS row.
Place Pocket
Cont in st st throughout, place pocket on next row as foll:
Next row (RS) K18 sts, slip next 27 sts onto a st holder, then with RS facing, K the 27 sts of the pocket lining from the st holder, K to end.
Work without shaping until Left Front measures 39cm (15¼") from beg, ending with a WS row.
Shape V-neck and Armhole
Beg V-neck shaping on next row as foll:
**Dec row (RS) K to last 5 sts, K2tog, K3.
P one row, K one row, P one row.
Rep dec row once.
P one row.**
Rep from ** to ** until there are 38 sts *and at the same time* when there are same number of rows as Back to armhole, cast (bind) off 10 sts at armhole edge (at beg of a RS row).
Work rem 38 sts without shaping until there are same number of rows as Back to shoulder, ending with a WS row.
Cast (bind) off.

RIGHT FRONT
Work as given for Left Front to ****.
Change to larger needles and work next row as foll:
Next row (RS) Rib the first 9 sts, then slip these 9 sts onto a st holder to be used later for front band, then K rem 73 sts.
Beg with a P row, cont in st st until there are same number of rows as Left Front to pocket, so ending with a WS row.

Place Pocket

Cont in st st throughout, place pocket on next row as foll:
Next row (RS) K28 sts, slip next 27 sts onto a st holder, then with RS facing, K the 27 sts of the pocket lining from the st holder, K to end.
Work without shaping until there are same number of rows as Left Front to neck shaping, so ending with a WS row.

Shape V-neck and Armhole

Beg V-neck shaping on next row as foll:
***Dec row** (RS) K3, sl 1-K1-psso, K to end.
P one row, K one row, P one row.
Rep dec row once.
P one row.***
Rep from *** to *** until there are 38 sts *and at the same time* when there are same number of rows as Back to armhole, cast (bind) off 10 sts at armhole edge (at beg of a WS row).
Work rem 38 sts without shaping until there are same number of

rows as Back to shoulder, ending with a RS row.
Cast (bind) off.

SLEEVES

Using smaller needles, cast on 52 sts.
Work 10cm (4") in K1, P1 rib as for Back, ending with a WS row.
Change to larger needles and beg with a K row, work in st st, inc one st at each end of 3rd row and every foll alt row until there are 116 sts.
Work in st st without shaping until Sleeve measures 44cm (17½") from beg or desired length, ending with a WS row.
Cast (bind) off all sts.
Make the 2nd Sleeve in the same way as the first.

LEFT FRONT BAND

Press pieces lightly on WS, following instructions on yarn label and omitting ribbing.
Join shoulder seams.
Using smaller needles and with

RS facing, work K1, P1 rib across 9 sts on st holder for front band on Left Front as foll:
1st rib row (RS) *P1, K1, rep from * to last 3 sts, P1, K2.
2nd rib row K1, *P1, K1, rep from * to end.
Rep last 2 rows until Band, when slightly stretched, fits up neck edge of Left Front to centre back neck.
Cast (bind) off in rib.

RIGHT FRONT BAND

Using smaller needles and with WS facing, work K1, P1 rib across 9 sts on st holder for front band on Right Front as foll:
1st rib row (WS) *P1, K1, rep from * to last 3 sts, P1, K2.
2nd rib row K1, *P1, K1, rep from * to end.
Rep last 2 rows until Band, when slightly stretched, fits up neck edge of Right Front to centre back neck.
Cast (bind) off in rib.

FINISHING

Sew Bands to centre edge of Fronts and join centre back seam.
Pocket Top
Using smaller needles and with RS of Left Front facing, work in K1, P1 rib across 27 sts from st holder at pocket top as given for Left Front Band.
Work 11 rows more in rib. Cast (bind) off in rib.
Work pocket top on Right Front in the same way.
Sew pocket linings neatly to WS of fronts. Sew ends of pocket tops to RS.
Placing centre of cast (bound) off sleeve edge at shoulder seam, sew cast (bound) off edge of Sleeves to vertical edge of armholes and sew cast (bound) off edge of armhole to sides of Sleeves.
Join side and sleeve seams.
Press seams lightly on WS, following instructions on yarn label and omitting ribbing.

JAZZ

SIZES
One size only (see page 107 for choosing size)
Finished measurement around bust 186cm (74")
See diagram for finished measurements of back, front and sleeves. To lengthen or shorten back and front, or sleeves see page 107.

MATERIALS
Wendy *Orinoco*
12 x 50g (1¾oz) balls in main colour — Sierra (shade no. 585) A
3 x 50g (1¾oz) balls each in Curzo (shade no. 587) B and Rio (shade no. 577) C
1 x 50g (1¾oz) ball each in Naranja (shade no. 583) D and Amapa (shade no. 570) G
2 x 50g (1¾oz) balls in Vino (shade no. 586) F
4 x 50g (1¾oz) balls each in El Dorado (shade no. 580) E and Poncho (shade no. 579) H
One pair each 5½mm (US size 9) and 6½mm (US size 10½) needles *or size to obtain correct tension (gauge)*
5½mm (US size 9) circular needle 40cm (16") long

TENSION (GAUGE)
14 sts and 20 rows to 10cm (4") over st st on 6½mm (US size 10½) needles
Check your tension (gauge) before beginning.

NOTES
Do not strand yarn across back of work, but use a separate ball for each isolated area of colour, twisting yarns at back when changing colours to avoid holes. Read charts from right to left for RS (knit) rows and from left to right for WS (purl) rows.

BACK
Using smaller needles and yarn A, cast on 130 sts.
Beg K2, P2 rib as foll:
1st rib row P1, *K2, P2, rep

from * to last st, K1.
Rep last row until ribbing measures 8cm (3¼") from beg, ending with a WS row.
Change to larger needles and beg with first chart row (K row), work in st st foll chart (page 61) for Back (see *Notes* above) until 146th row has been completed, so ending with a WS row.
Shape Neck
Beg neck shaping on next row as foll:
147th chart row (RS) Work 47 sts in patt, turn leaving rem sts on a spare needle.
Working on first side of neck only and cont to foll chart for patt, dec one st at neck edge on every row 3 times. 44 sts.
Cast (bind) off.
Return to rem sts and with RS facing, slip centre 36 sts onto a st holder, rejoin yarn to rem sts and work in patt to end of row.
Complete 2nd side of neck to match first side, reversing all shaping.

FRONT
Work as for Back until 130th

chart row has been completed, so ending with a WS row.
Shape Neck
Beg neck shaping on next row as foll:
131st chart row (RS) Work 54 sts in patt, turn leaving rem sts on a spare needle.
Working on first side of neck only and cont to foll chart for patt throughout, cast (bind) off 2 sts at beg of next row and foll alt row, then dec one st at neck edge on every row 6 times, so ending with a WS row. 44 sts.
Work 10 rows without shaping.
Cast (bind) off.
Return to rem sts and with RS facing, slip centre 22 sts onto a st holder, rejoin yarn to rem sts and work in patt to end of row.
Cont to foll chart for patt throughout, work one row without shaping.
Cast (bind) off 2 sts at beg of next row and foll alt row, then dec one st at neck edge on every row 6 times, so ending with a RS row. 44 sts.
Work 9 rows without shaping.
Cast (bind) off.

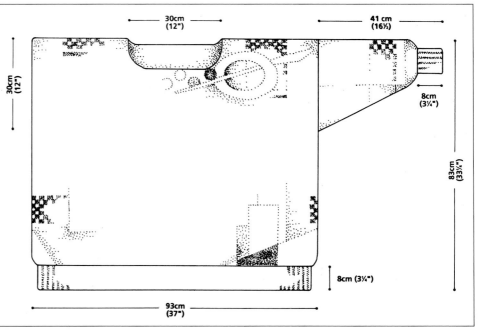

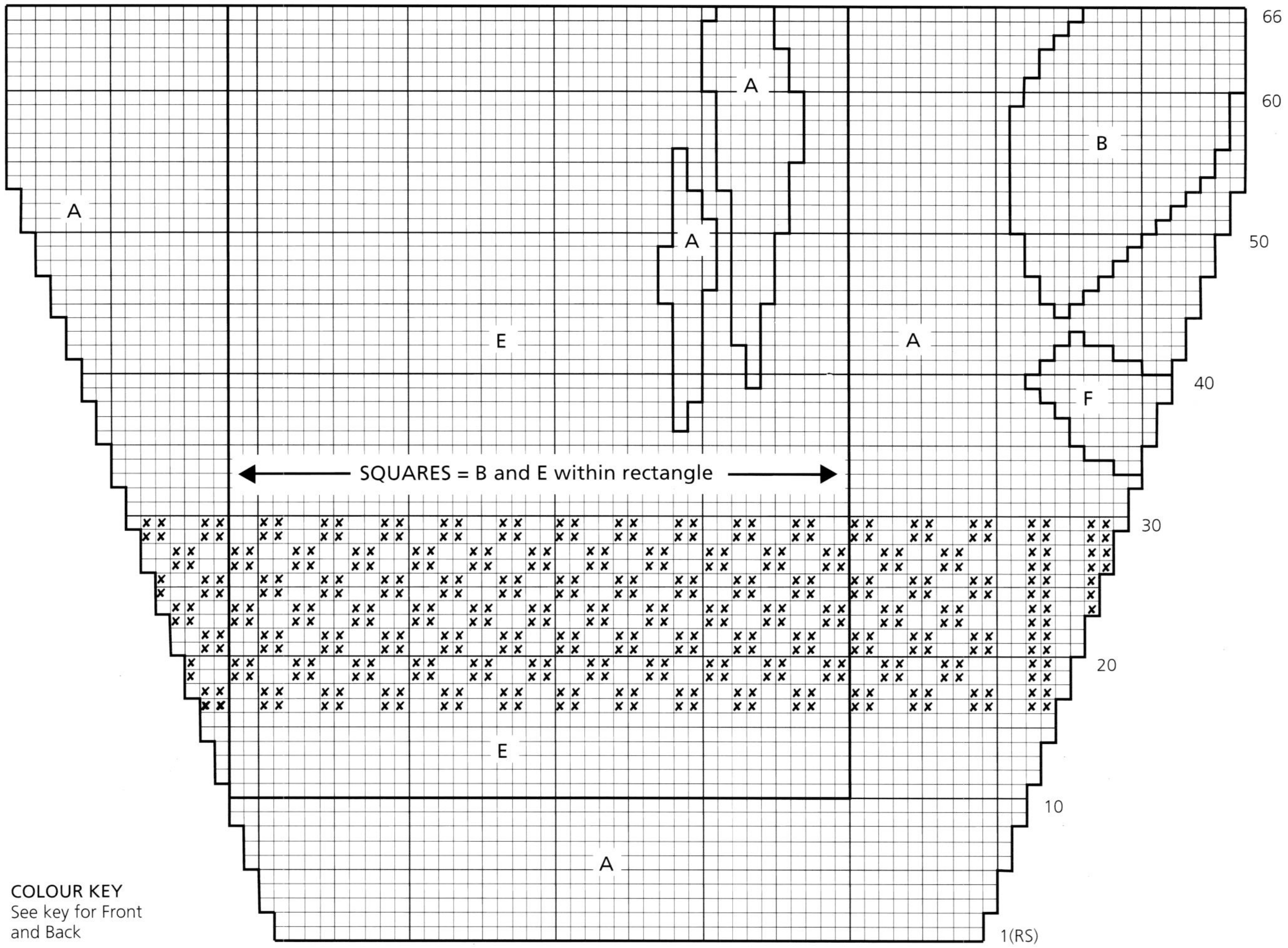

SQUARES = B and E within rectangle

COLOUR KEY
See key for Front
and Back

SLEEVE CHART

SLEEVES

Using smaller needles and yarn A,
cast on 38 sts.
Beg K2, P2 rib as foll:
1st rib row (RS) K1, *P2, K2, rep
from * to last st, P1.
Rep last row until ribbing
measures 8cm (3¼") from beg,
ending with a RS row.
Inc 10 sts evenly across next row
as foll:
Next row (inc row) (WS) K into
front and back of first st, *P2,
K1, K into front and back of next
st, rep from * to last st, P1.
48 sts.
Change to larger needles and
beg with a K row, work 2 rows in

st st. Cont in st st throughout, inc
one st at each end of next row,
then inc one st at each end of
every foll 3rd row twice, so
ending with a RS row. 54 sts.
Work one row without shaping.
Then beg with 11th chart row,
foll chart for Sleeve *and at the
same time* cont shaping Sleeve as
before by inc one st at each end
of every 3rd row until there are
84 sts, so ending with a WS row.
Work 12 rows in patt without
shaping or work to desired
length.
Cast (bind) off all sts *loosely*.
Make the 2nd Sleeve in the same
way as the first.

COLLAR

Press pieces lightly on WS,
following instructions on yarn
label and omitting ribbing.
Join right and left shoulder
seams.
Using circular needle and yarn H
(purple) and with RS facing, beg
at right shoulder seam, pick up
and K3 sts down right back neck,
K36 sts from back neck st holder,
pick up and K3 sts up left back
neck and 16 sts down left front
neck, K22 sts from front neck st
holder and pick up and K16 sts
up right front neck. 96 sts.
Working in rounds with RS
always facing and marking beg of

TENNESSEE

SIZE

One size only (see page 107 for choosing size)
Finished measurement around bust 150cm (60")
See diagram for finished measurements of back, front and sleeves. To lengthen or shorten back and front, or sleeves see page 107.

MATERIALS

28 x 50g (1¾oz) balls of Rowan *Den-m-nit Indigo Dyed DK* (see *Note* below about shrinkage) in Tennessee (shade no. 230)
One pair each 3¼mm (US size 3) and 4mm (US size 6) needles *or size to obtain correct tension (gauge)*
4 stitch markers (see *Notes*)

TENSION (GAUGE)

19 sts and 34 rows to 10cm (4") over moss (seed) st after washing (see *Notes* below) on 4mm (US size 6) needles
Check your tension (gauge) before beginning.

NOTES

When washed for the first time this yarn will shrink by up to one fifth in length; however, the width will remain the same. Read the yarn label for the washing instructions.
Three different st patts are worked in panels across the Back and Front (and two across the Sleeves). Instructions are given for placing st markers between the panels. These st markers are slipped in each row so that they are always positioned on the needles between the panels as a guide for the knitter. An experienced knitter may not find the st markers necessary.

MOSS (SEED) STITCH

The foll instructions are for working moss (seed) st over an even number of sts.
1st row (RS) *K1, P1, rep from * to end.
2nd row *P1, K1, rep from * to end.
The last 2 rows are repeated to form the moss (seed) st patt over an even number of sts.
The foll instructions are for working moss (seed) st over an odd number of sts.
1st row (RS) P1, *K1, P1, rep from * to end.
The last row is repeated to form the moss (seed) st patt over an odd number of sts.

ZIGZAG PANEL

This panel is worked over 15 sts.
1st row (RS) K1, P2, K2, take yarn to front between two needles, then take yarn from front to back over top of RH needle to make a new loop — called *yarn over* or *yo* —, sl 1-K1-psso, K5, P2, K1.
2nd row and foll WS rows P1, K2, P9, K2, P1.
3rd row K1, P2, K3, yo, sl 1-K1-psso, K4, P2, K1.
5th row K1, P2, K4, yo, sl 1-K1-psso, K3, P2, K1.
7th row K1, P2, K5, yo, sl 1-K1-psso, K2, P2, K1.
9th row K1, P2, K2, yo, sl 1-K1-psso, K2, yo, sl 1-K1-psso, K1, P2, K1.
11th row K1, P2, K1, (yo, sl 1-K1-psso) twice, K2, yo, sl 1-K1-psso, P2, K1.
13th row K1, P2, K2, yo, sl 1-K1-psso, K2, K2tog, yo, K1, P2, K1.
14th row As 2nd row.
These 14 rows are repeated to form the zigzag patt.

LOZENGE LACE PANEL

This panel is worked over 17 sts.
1st row (RS) P3, K1, yo, sl 1-K1-psso, K5, K2tog, yo, K1, P3.
2nd row and foll WS rows K3, P11, K3.
3rd row P3, K2, yo, sl 1-K1-psso, K3, K2tog, yo, K2, P3.
5th row P3, K3, yo, sl 1-K1-psso, K1, K2tog, yo, K3, P3.
7th row P3, K4, yo, sl 1-K2tog-psso, yo, K4, P3.
9th row P3, K3, K2tog, yo, K1, yo, sl 1-K1-psso, K3, P3.
11th row P3, K2, K2tog, yo, K3, yo, sl 1-K1-psso, K2, P3.

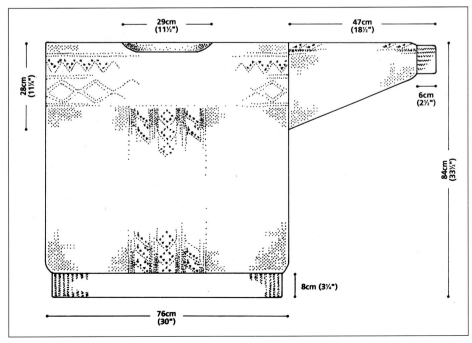

Baggy, easy to wear, fantastic.

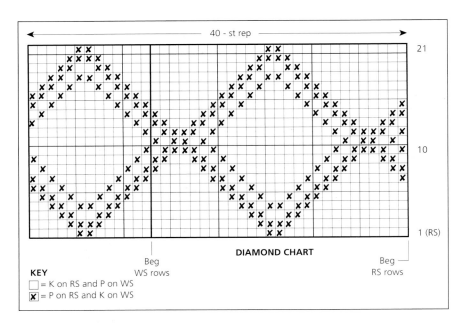

40 - st rep

21

10

1 (RS)

DIAMOND CHART

Beg
WS rows

Beg
RS rows

KEY
☐ = K on RS and P on WS
☒ = P on RS and K on WS

13th row P3, K1, K2tog, yo, K5, yo, sl 1-K1-psso, K1, P3.
15th row P3, K2tog, yo, K7, yo, sl 1-K1-psso, P3.
16th row As 2nd row.
These 16 rows are repeated to form the lozenge lace patt.

LACE CHEVRON STITCH PATTERN
This st patt is worked over a multiple of 20 sts plus 7 extra.
1st row (RS) K9, *yo, sl next 2 sts knitwise (one at a time) onto RH needle, insert tip of LH needle into fronts of 2 slipped sts and knit them tog — called *slip, slip, knit* or *ssk* —, K8, rep from *, ending last rep K6 instead of K8.
2nd row and foll WS rows Purl.
3rd row K7, *K2tog, yo, K1, yo, ssk, K5, rep from * to end.
5th row K6, *K2tog, yo, K3, yo, ssk, K3, rep from *, ending last rep K4 instead of K3.
7th row K5, *K2tog, yo, K5, yo, ssk, K1, rep from *, ending last rep K3 instead of K1.
9th row K4, K2tog, yo, K7, *yo, sl 1-K2tog-psso, yo, K7, rep from * to last 4 sts, yo, ssk, K2.
10th row As 2nd row.
These 10 rows form the lace chevron st patt.

BACK
Using smaller needles, cast on 147 sts.
Beg K1, P1, rib as foll:
1st rib row (RS) P1, *K1, P1, rep from * to end.
2nd rib row K1, *P1, K1, rep from * to end.
Rep last 2 rows 12 times more, so ending with a WS row.
Change to larger needles and position patt sts across Back (see *Notes* above) as foll:
1st patt row (RS) Work first row of moss (seed) st over first 50 sts and slip st marker onto RH needle; work first row of zigzag panel over next 15 sts and slip on st marker; work first row of lozenge lace panel over next 17 sts and slip on st marker; work first row of zigzag panel over next 15 sts and slip on st marker; work first row of moss (seed) st over last 50 sts.
2nd patt row Work 2nd row of moss (seed) st over first 50 sts and slip marker; work 2nd row of zigzag panel over next 15 sts and slip marker; work 2nd row of lozenge lace panel over next 17 sts and slip marker; work 2nd row of zigzag panel over next 15 sts and slip marker; work 2nd

row of moss (seed) st over last 50 sts.
Cont in patt as set (working moss (seed) st, lozenge lace and zigzag panels between markers foll row by row instructions) until 186 patt rows have been worked (see *Notes* above about shrinkage of yarn), ending with a WS row. This completes panels.
K one row.
P one row.
K 5 rows.
P one row, so ending with a WS row.
Beg with first chart row (RS row), work diamond patt across all 147 sts, foll 40-st rep on diamond chart until 21st chart row has been completed, so ending with a RS row.
P one row.
K 5 rows.
Beg with a P row, work 5 rows in st st, so ending with a WS row.
Beg with a first patt row, work the 10 rows of lace chevron patt across all sts, so ending with a WS row.
K one row.
P one row.
K 5 rows, so ending with a RS row.**
Work 13 rows in moss (seed) st, so ending with a WS row.
Keeping moss (seed) st correct, cast (bind) off 46 sts at beg of next 2 rows.
Slip rem 55 sts onto a st holder for back neck.

FRONT
Work as for Back to **.
Work one row in moss (seed) st, so ending with a WS row.
Shape Neck
Keeping moss (seed) st correct throughout, beg neck shaping on next row as foll:
Next row (RS) Work 56 sts in moss (seed) st, turn leaving rem sts on a spare needle.
Working on first side of neck only, dec one st at neck edge on next 10 rows. 46 sts.
Work one row without shaping.

Cast (bind) off.
Return to rem sts and with RS facing, slip centre 35 sts onto a st holder, then rejoin yarn and work in moss (seed) st to end of row. Dec one st at neck edge on next 10 rows. 46 sts.
Work 2 rows without shaping. Cast (bind) off.

SLEEVES
Using smaller needles, cast on 47 sts.
Work 22 rows in K1, P1 rib as for Back, ending with a WS row.
Change to larger needles and position patt sts as foll:
1st patt row (RS) Work first row of moss (seed) st over first 16 sts and slip st marker onto RH needle; work first row of zigzag panel over next 15 sts and slip on st marker; work first row of moss (seed) st over last 16 sts.

2nd patt row Work 2nd row of moss (seed) st over first 16 sts and slip marker; work 2nd row of zigzag panel over next 15 sts and slip marker; work 2nd row of moss (seed) st over last 16 sts.
Cont in patt as set, inc one st at each end of next row and every foll alt row until there are 111 sts *and at the same time* work all extra sts outside first and last st markers in moss (seed) st.
Work in patt without shaping until 136 patt rows have been worked (see *Notes* above about yarn shrinkage), ending with a WS row.
Cast (bind) off all sts in patt. Make the 2nd Sleeve in the same way as the first.

COLLAR
Wash and dry the *Den-m-nit Cotton* pieces foll instructions on yarn label (see *Notes* on page 62).
Join right shoulder seam.
Using smaller needles and with RS facing, pick up and K8 sts down left front neck, K35 sts from front neck st holder, pick up and K8 sts up right front neck and K55 sts from back neck st holder. 106 sts.
Work 5cm (2") in K1, P1 rib.
Cast (bind) off in rib.

FINISHING
Join left shoulder seam and collar.
Placing centre of cast (bound) off sleeve edge at shoulder seam, sew Sleeves to Back and Fronts, matching sides.
Join side and sleeve seams.
Press seams lightly on WS with a warm iron over a damp cloth, omitting ribbing.

MATISSE KING

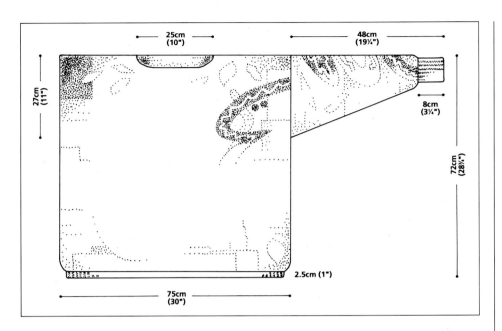

SIZE
One size only (see page 107 for choosing size)
Finished measurement around bust 150cm (60")
See diagram for finished measurements of back, front and sleeves. To lengthen or shorten back and front, or sleeves see page 107.

MATERIALS
Rowan *Handknit DK Cotton*
10 x 50g (1¾oz) balls in Royal (shade no. 294) A
3 x 50g (1¾oz) balls each in Black (shade no. 252) B and Purple (shade no. 272) C
2 x 50g (1¾oz) balls in Yellow (shade no. 271) D
4 x 50g (1¾oz) balls in Azure Green (shade no. 248) E
1 x 50g (1¾oz) ball each in Mango (shade no. 262) F, Ecru (shade no. 251) G and Spring Green (shade no. 274) H
One pair each 3¼mm (US size 3) and 4mm (US size 6) needles *or size to obtain correct tension (gauge)*

TENSION (GAUGE)
20 sts and 28 rows to 10cm (4") over st st on 4mm (US size 6) needles
Check your tension (gauge) before beginning.

NOTES
Do not strand yarn across back of work, but use a separate ball or length of yarn for each isolated area of colour, twisting yarns at back when changing colours to avoid holes.
Read charts from right to left for RS (knit) rows and from left to right for WS (purl) rows.

BACK
Using smaller needles and yarn A, cast on 150 sts.
Beg K1, P1 rib as foll:
1st rib row (RS) *K1, P1, rep from * to end.
Rep last row until ribbing

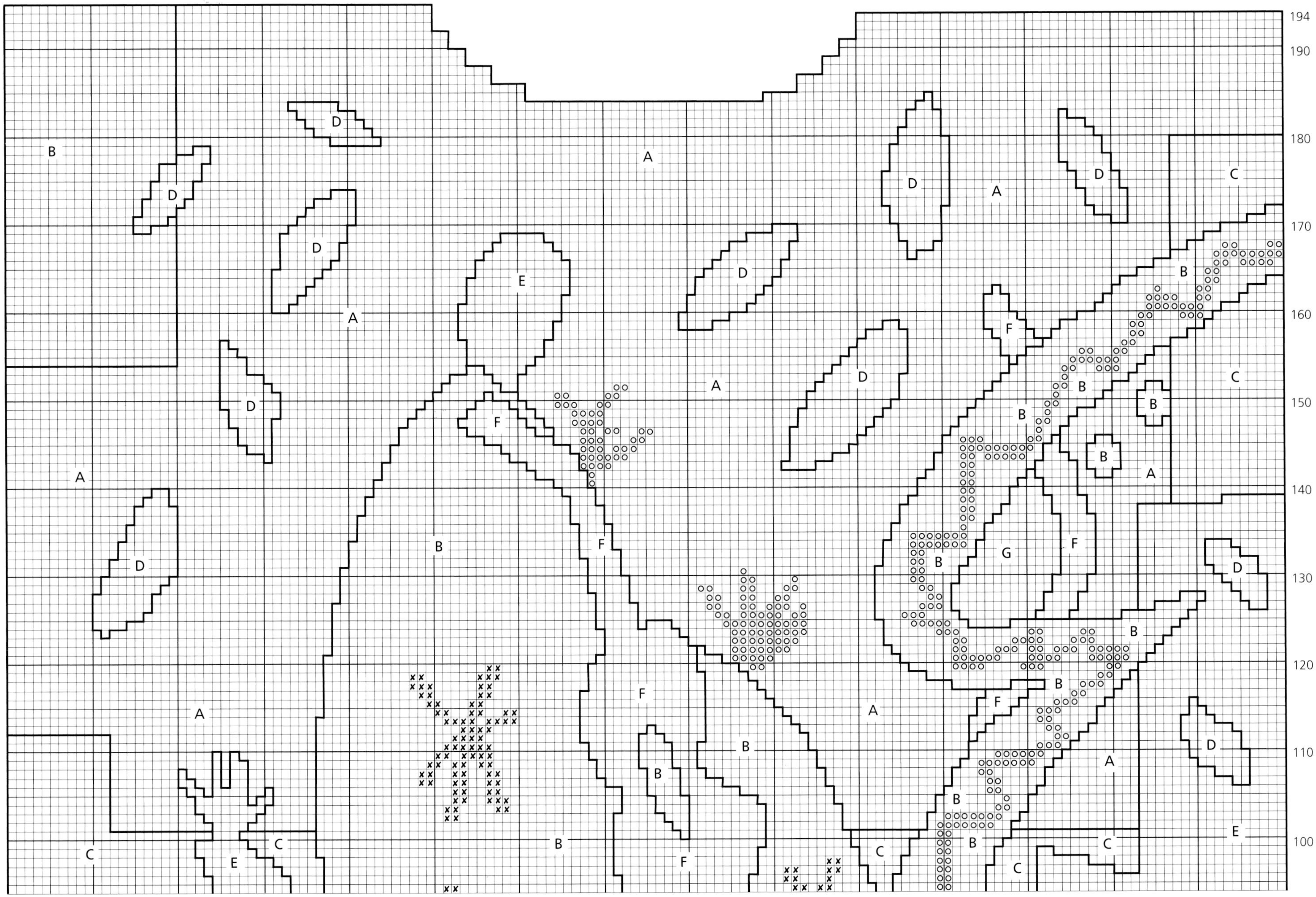

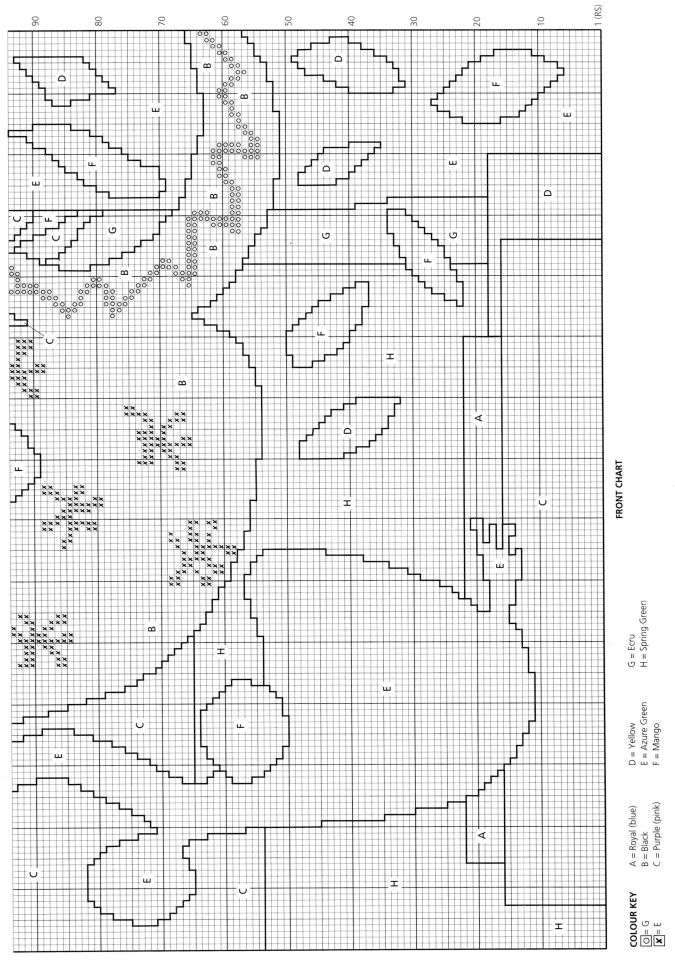

FRONT CHART

COLOUR KEY

A = Royal (blue)	D = Yellow	G = Ecru
B = Black	E = Azure Green	H = Spring Green
C = Purple (pink)	F = Mango	

○ = G
☒ = E

69

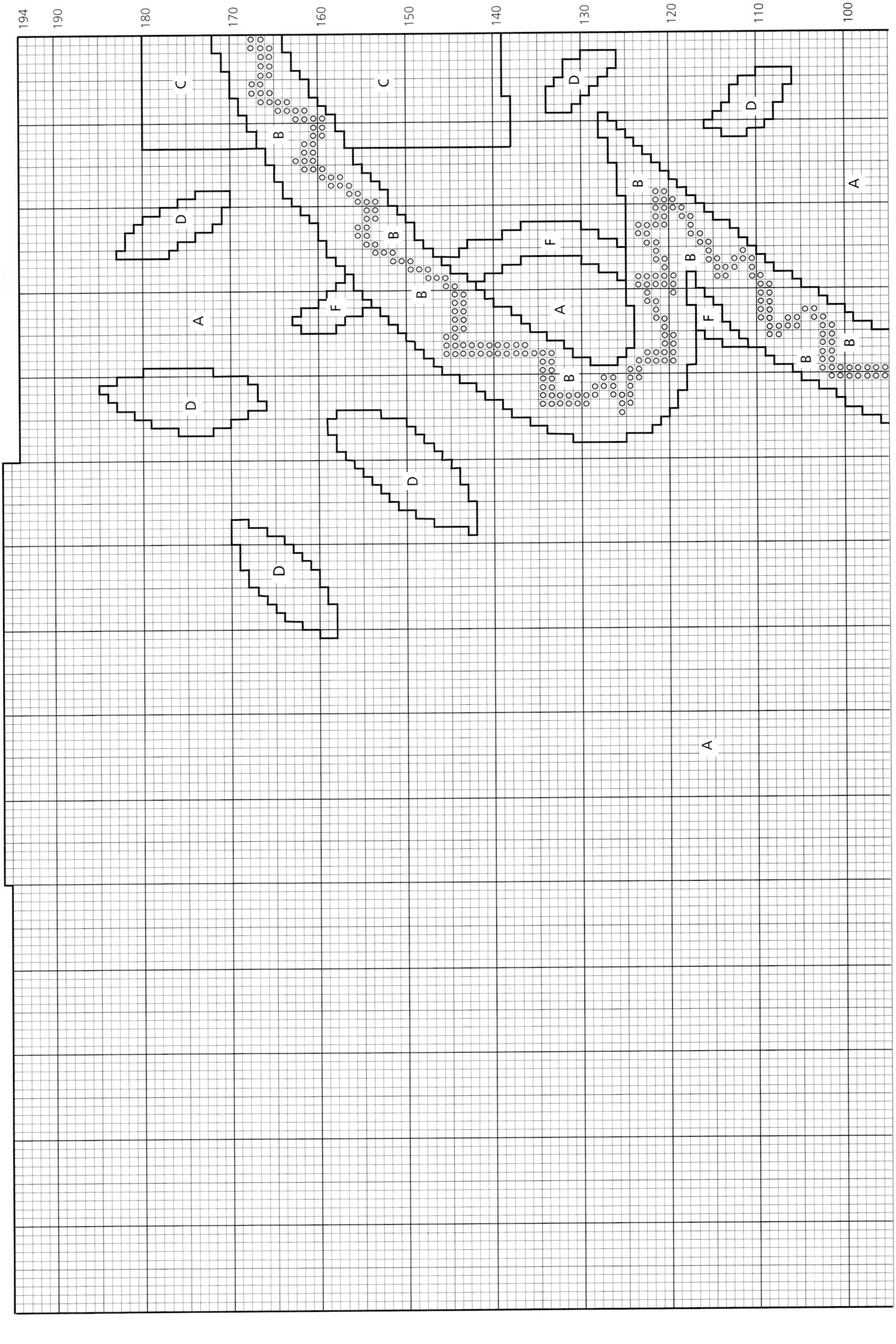

C

C

D

D

A

D

B

B

B

F

B

B

A

A

F

D

B

F

B

A

D

D

A

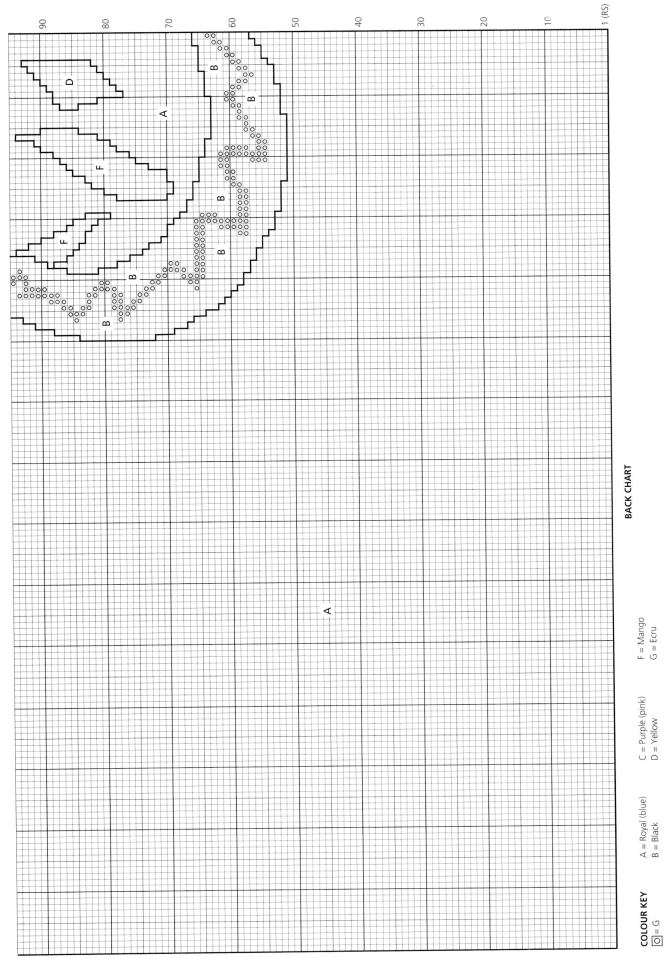

BACK CHART

COLOUR KEY

◯ = G

A = Royal (blue)
B = Black

C = Purple (pink)
D = Yellow

F = Mango
G = Ecru

71

measures 2.5cm (1") from beg, ending with a WS row.**
Change to larger needles and beg with a K row, work 51 rows in st st, so ending with a RS row. Beg with 52nd chart row (P row), cont in st st foll chart (page 71) for Back (see *Notes*) until 194th row has been completed, so

ending with a WS row.
Using A only and cont in st st, cast (bind) off 50 sts at beg of next 2 rows.
Slip rem 50 sts onto a st holder for back neck.

FRONT
Work as for Back to **.

Change to larger needles and beg with first chart row (K row), work in st st foll chart (page 69) for Front until 184th chart row has been completed, so ending with a WS row.
Shape Neck
Cont to foll chart for colour patt and working in st st throughout,

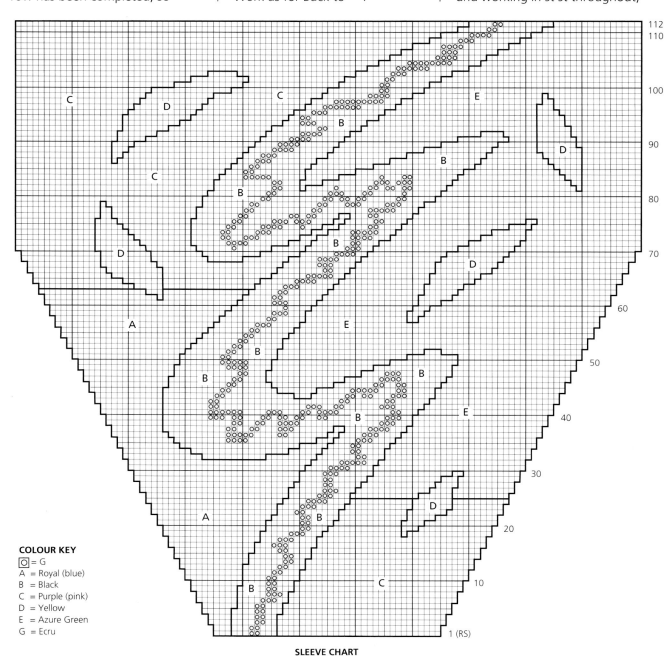

COLOUR KEY
⊡ = G
A = Royal (blue)
B = Black
C = Purple (pink)
D = Yellow
E = Azure Green
G = Ecru

SLEEVE CHART

beg of foll alt row, then 2 sts at beg of 2 foll alt rows. 50 sts.
Work 2 rows without shaping, so ending with a RS row.
Cast (bind) off.

SLEEVES

Using smaller needles and yarn A, cast on 40 sts.
Work 8cm (3¼") in K1, P1 rib as for Back, ending with a WS row.
Change to larger needles and beg with first chart row (K row), work in st st foll chart for Sleeve *and at the same time* shape Sleeve by inc one st at each end of 3rd row and then every foll alt row until there are 110 sts, so ending with a RS row.
Cont to foll chart for colour patt and working in st st throughout, work without shaping until 112th chart row has been completed or until Sleeve is desired length, ending with a WS row.
Cast (bind) off all sts.
Make the 2nd Sleeve in the same way as the first.

NECKBAND

Press pieces lightly on WS with a warm iron over a damp cloth, omitting ribbing.
Join right shoulder seam.
Using smaller needles and yarn A and with RS facing, pick up and K19 sts down left front neck, K28 sts from front neck st holder, pick up and K19 sts up right front neck and K50 sts from back neck st holder. 116 sts.
Work 2.5cm (1") in K1, P1 rib as for Back.
Cast (bind) off in rib.

FINISHING

Join left shoulder seam and neckband.
Placing centre of cast (bound) off sleeve edge at shoulder seam, sew Sleeves to Back and Front, matching sides.
Join side and sleeve seams.
Press seams lightly on WS with a warm iron over a damp cloth, omitting ribbing.

beg neck shaping on next row as foll:
185th chart row (RS) Work 61 sts in patt, turn leaving rem sts on a spare needle.
Working on first side of neck only, cast (bind) off 4 sts at beg of next row, cast (bind) off 3 sts at beg of foll alt row, then 2 sts at beg of 2 foll alt rows. 50 sts.

Work 2 rows without shaping, so ending with a WS row.
Cast (bind) off.
Return to rem sts and with RS facing, slip centre 28 sts onto a st holder, then rejoin yarn and work in patt to end of row.
Work one row without shaping.
Cast (bind) off 4 sts at beg of next row, cast (bind) off 3 sts at

PICASSO

(diagram with measurements: 23cm (9¼"), 46cm (18"), 31cm (12¼"), 5cm (2"), 77cm (30½"), 5cm (2"), 73cm (29¼"))

SIZE
One size only (see page 107 for choosing size)
Finished measurement around bust 146cm (58½")
See diagram for finished measurements of back, front and sleeves. To lengthen or shorten back and front, or sleeves see page 107.

MATERIALS
Rowan *Handknit DK Cotton*
16 x 50g (1¾oz) balls in main colour — Black (shade no. 252) A
3 x 50g (1¾oz) balls each in Ecru (no. 251) B, Scarlet (shade no. 255) C, Peacock (shade no. 259) D and Bathstone (shade no. 257) E
One pair each 3¼mm (US size 3) and 4mm (US size 6) needles *or size to obtain correct tension (gauge)*

TENSION (GAUGE)
20 sts and 28 rows to 10cm (4") over st st on 4mm (US size 6) needles
Check your tension (gauge) before beginning.

NOTES
Do not strand yarn across back of work, but use a separate ball or length of yarn for each isolated area of colour, twisting yarns at back when changing colours to avoid holes.
Read chart from right to left for RS (knit) rows and from left to right for WS (purl) rows.

BACK
Using smaller needles and yarn A, cast on 146 sts.
Beg K2, P2 rib as foll:
1st rib row (RS) P1, *K2, P2, rep from * to last st, K1.
Rep last row until ribbing measures 5cm (2") from beg, ending with a WS row.**
Change to larger needles and beg with a K row, work 200 rows in st st.
Cast (bind) off 50 sts at beg of next 2 rows.
Slip rem 46 sts onto a st holder for back neck.

FRONT
Work as for Back to **.
Change to larger needles and beg with a K row, work 20 rows in st st, so ending with a WS row.
Beg with 21st chart row, work in st st foll chart (page 77) for Front (see *Notes* above) until 160th chart row has been completed, so ending with a WS row.
Shape Neck
Beg neck shaping on next row as foll:
161st chart row (RS) Work 63 sts in patt, turn leaving rem sts on a spare needle.
Working on first side of neck only and cont in st st throughout, cast (bind) off 2 sts at beg of next row and every foll alt row 5 times in all, then dec one st at beg of 3 foll alt rows. 50 sts.
Work 24 rows without shaping.
Cast (bind) off.
Return to rem st and with RS facing, slip centre 20 sts onto a st holder, rejoin yarn to rem sts and work in patt to end.
Work one row in patt.
Cont to foll chart for patt, cast (bind) off 2 sts at beg of next row and every foll alt row 5 times in all, then dec one st at beg of 3 foll alt rows. 50 sts.
Work 24 rows without shaping.
Cast (bind) off.

SLEEVES
Using smaller needles and yarn A, cast on 50 sts.
Work 5cm (2") in K2, P2 rib as for Back, ending with a WS row.
Change to larger needles and beg with a K row, work in st st, inc one st at each end of next

row and every foll alt row until
there are 126 sts.
Cont in st st without shaping
until Sleeve measures 46cm (18")
from beg or desired length,
ending with a WS row.
Cast (bind) off all sts.
Make the 2nd Sleeve in the same
way as the first.

NECKBAND
Press pieces lightly on WS with a
warm iron over a damp cloth,
omitting ribbing.
Join right shoulder seam.
Using smaller needles and yarn A
and with RS facing, pick up and
K30 down left front neck, K20 sts
from front neck st holder, pick up
and K30 sts up right front neck
and K46 sts from back neck st
holder. 126 sts.
Work 4cm (1½") in K2, P2 rib as
for Back. Cast (bind) off in rib.

FINISHING
Join left shoulder seam and
neckband.
Placing centre of cast (bound) off
sleeve edge at shoulder seam,
sew Sleeves to Back and Front,
matching sides.
Join the side and the sleeve
seams.
Press seams lightly on WS with a
warm iron over a damp cloth,
omitting ribbing.

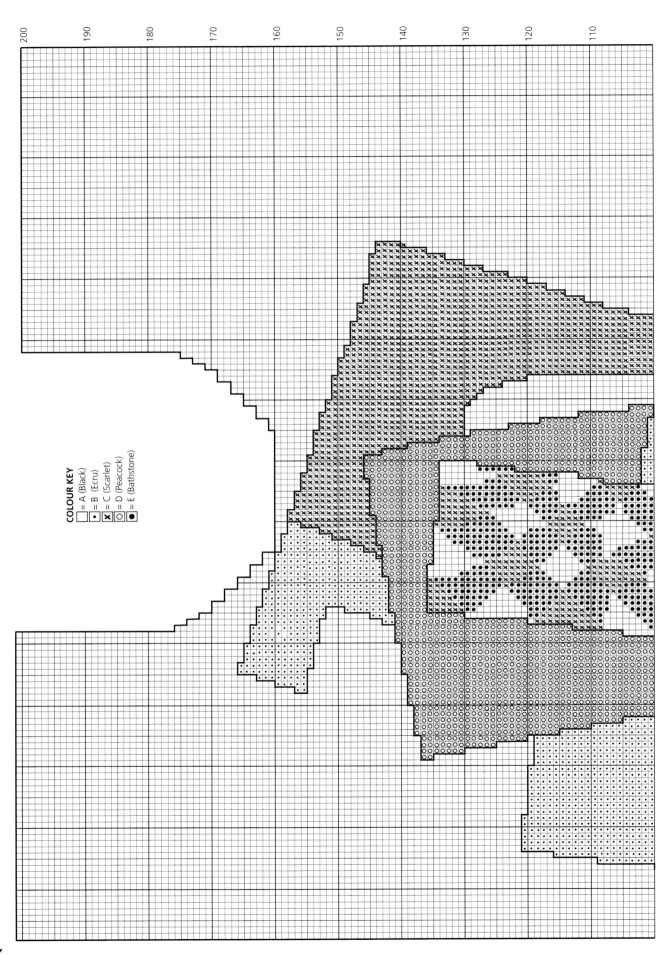

COLOUR KEY

☐ = A (Black)
· = B (Ecru)
✗ = C (Scarlet)
◯ = D (Peacock)
● = E (Bathstone)

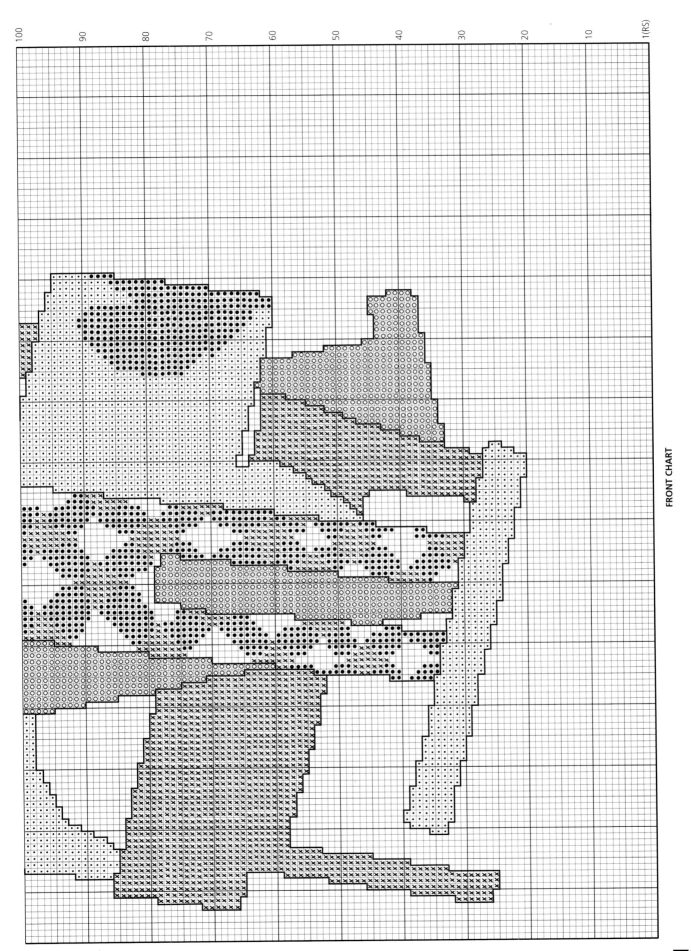

FRONT CHART

Not just a jumper – a work of art.

MIRO

SIZE
One size only (see page 107 for choosing size)
Finished measurement around bust 150cm (60")
See diagram for finished measurements of back, front and sleeves. To lengthen or shorten back and front, or sleeves see page 107.

MATERIALS
Rowan *Handknit DK Cotton*
16 x 50g (1¾oz) balls in main colour — China (shade no. 267) A
6 x 50g (1¾oz) balls in Black (shade no. 252) B
1 x 50g (1¾oz) ball each in Sunflower (shade no. 261) C and Pimpernel (shade no. 249) D
One pair each 3¼mm (US size 3) and 4mm (US size 6) needles *or size to obtain correct tension (gauge)*

TENSION (GAUGE)
20 sts and 28 rows to 10cm (4") over st st on 4mm (US size 6) needles
Check your tension (gauge) before beginning.

NOTES
Do not strand yarn across back of work, but use a separate ball or length of yarn for each isolated area of colour, twisting yarns at back when changing colours to avoid holes.
Read charts from right to left for RS (knit) rows and from left to right for WS (purl) rows.

BACK
Using smaller needles and yarn B, cast on 150 sts.
Beg K1, P1 rib as foll:
1st rib row (RS) *K1, P1, rep from * to end.
Rep last row until ribbing measures 5cm (2") from beg, ending with a WS row.
Change to larger needles and beg with first chart row (K row), work in st st foll chart (page 83)

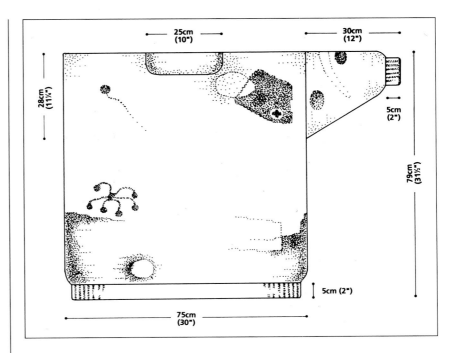

for Back (see *Notes*) until 206th row has been completed, so ending with a WS row.
Using A, cast (bind) off 50 sts at beg of next 2 rows.
Slip rem 50 sts onto a st holder for back neck.

FRONT
Work as for Back to until 186th chart row has been completed, so ending with a WS row.
Shape Neck
Using A only, beg neck shaping on next row as foll:
187th chart row (RS) K56, turn leaving rem sts on a spare needle. Working on first side of neck only and cont in st st throughout, dec one st at neck edge on every row 4 times, then dec one st at neck edge on 2 foll alt rows. 50 sts.
Work 11 rows without shaping, so ending at side edge.
Cast (bind) off.
Return to rem sts and with RS facing, slip centre 38 sts onto a st holder, rejoin yarn to rem sts and K to end of row.
Complete 2nd side of neck to match first side, reversing all shaping.

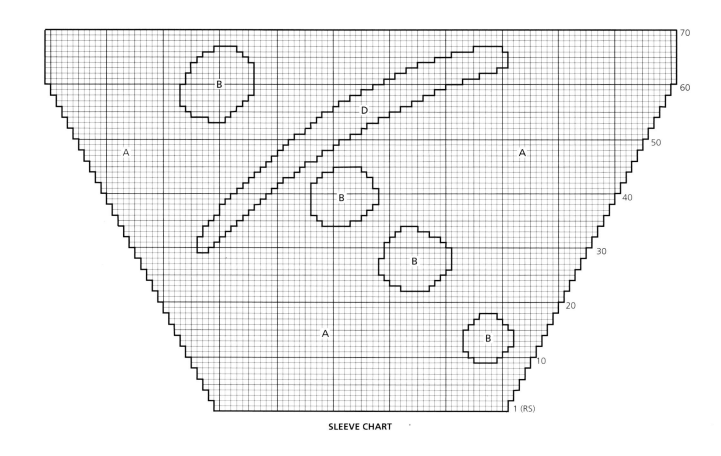

SLEEVE CHART

COLOUR KEY
X = B
A = China (blue)
B = Black
C = Sunflower (yellow)
D = Pimpernel (red)

SLEEVES
Using smaller needles and yarn B, cast on 52 sts.
Change to yarn A and work 5cm (2″) in K1, P1 rib as for Back, ending with a WS row.
Change to larger needles and beg with first chart row (K row), work in st st foll chart for Sleeve *and at the same time* shape Sleeve by inc one st at each end of 3rd row and then every foll alt row until there are 112 sts, so ending with a RS row.
Work 9 rows in patt without shaping.
Cast (bind) off all sts.

Make the 2nd Sleeve in the same way as the first.

COLLAR
Press pieces lightly on WS with a warm iron over a damp cloth, omitting ribbing.
Join right shoulder seam.
Using smaller needles and yarn A and with RS facing, pick up and K18 down left front neck, K38 sts from front neck st holder, pick up and K18 sts up right front neck and K50 sts from back neck st holder. 124 sts.
Beg K2, P2 rib as foll:
1st rib row (WS) *K2, P2, rep from * to the end of the row.
Rep last row until Collar measures 10cm (4″) from beg, working last row in D.
Still using D, cast (bind) off in rib.

FINISHING
Join left shoulder seam and collar.
Placing centre of cast (bound) off sleeve edge at shoulder seam, sew Sleeves to Back and Front, matching sides.
Join side and sleeve seams.
Press seams lightly on WS with a warm iron over a damp cloth, omitting ribbing.

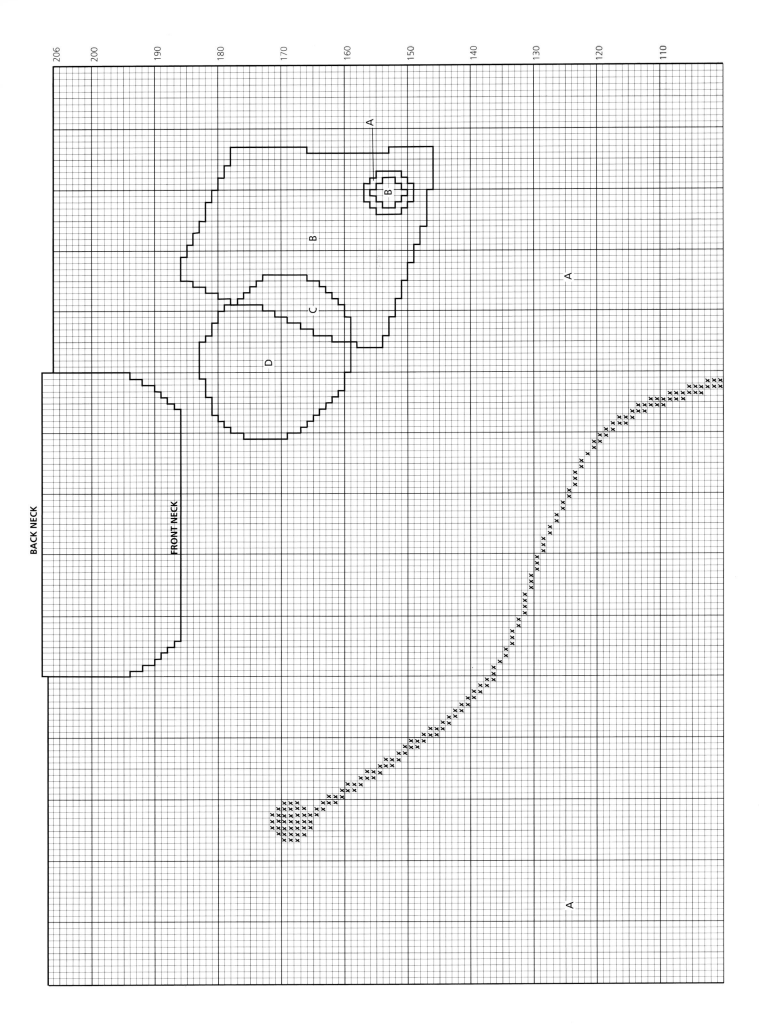

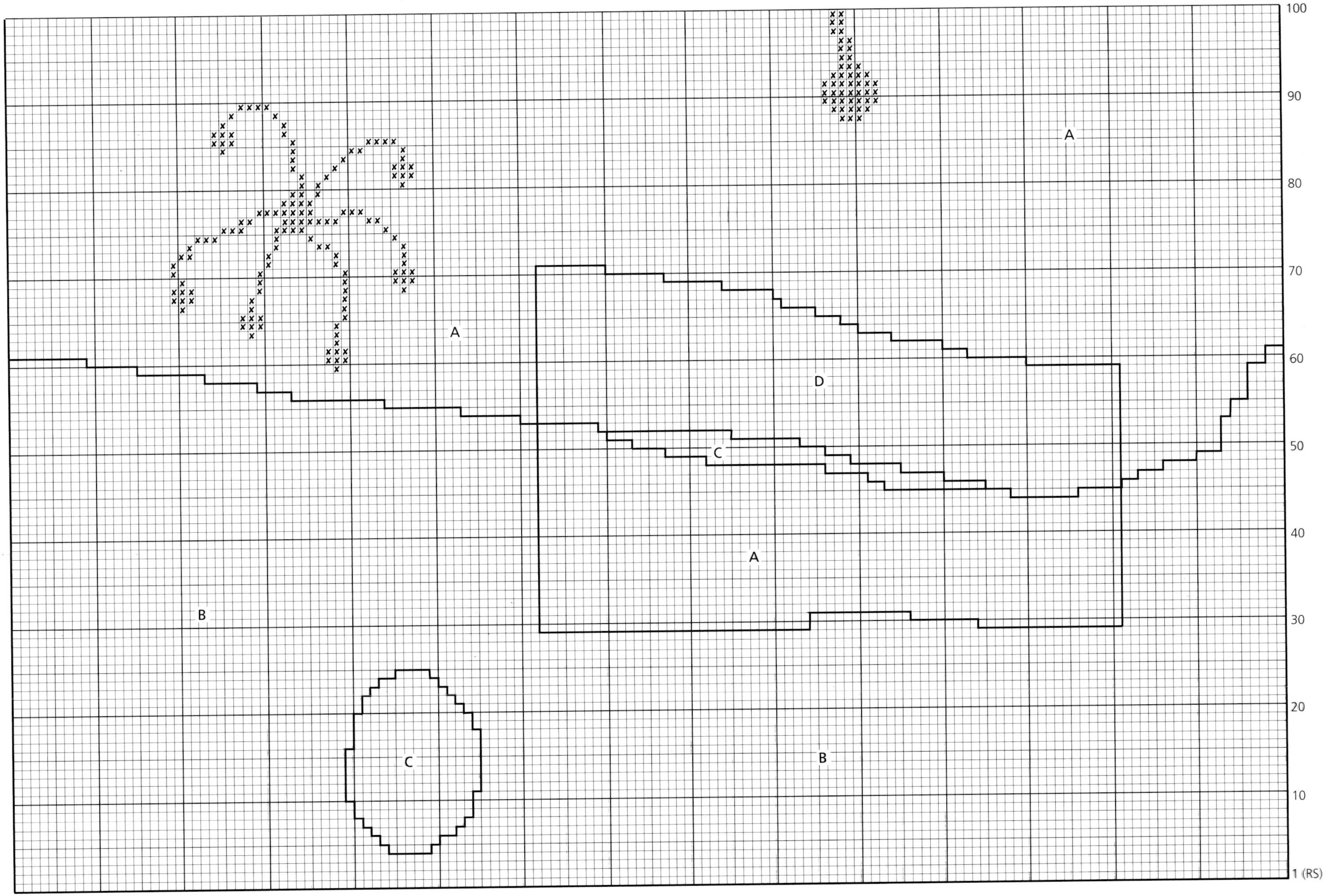

FRONT AND BACK CHART

See page 80 for Colour Key

Frame all three and hang them in the National Gallery immediately (the jumpers, not the models).

85

ART DECO

SIZE

One size only (see page 107 for choosing size)
Finished measurement around bust 150cm (60")
See diagram for finished measurements of back, front and sleeves. To lengthen or shorten back and front, or sleeves see page 107.

MATERIALS

Rowan *Handknit DK Cotton*
8 x 50g (1¾oz) balls each in Black (shade no. 252) A and Mustard (shade no. 246) B
4 x 50g (1¾oz) balls in Clover (shade no. 266) C
2 x 50g (1¾oz) ball in Pimpernel (shade no. 249) D
3 x 50g (1¾oz) ball in Nut (shade no. 297) E
One pair each 3¼mm (US size 3) and 4mm (US size 6) needles *or size to obtain correct tension (gauge)*

TENSION (GAUGE)

20 sts and 28 rows to 10cm (4") over st st on 4mm (US size 6) needles
Check your tension (gauge) before beginning.

NOTES

Do not strand yarn across back of work, but use a separate ball or length of yarn for each isolated area of colour, twisting yarns at back when changing colours to avoid holes.
Read charts from right to left for RS (knit) rows and from left to right for WS (purl) rows.

BACK

Using smaller needles and yarn A, cast on 150 sts.
Beg K1, P1 rib as foll:
1st rib row (RS) *K1, P1, rep from * to end.
Rep last row until ribbing measures 2.5cm (1") from beg, ending with a WS row.
Change to larger needles and beg with first chart row (K row), work in st st foll chart (page 91) for Back (see *Notes*) until 196th row has been completed, so ending with a WS row.
Shape Neck
Cont to foll chart for colour patt and working in st st throughout, beg neck shaping on next row as foll:
197th chart row (RS) Work 61 sts in patt, turn leaving rem sts on a spare needle.
Working on first side of neck only, cast (bind) off 6 sts beg of next row, then cast (bind) off 5 sts at beg of foll alt row.
Cast (bind) off rem 50 sts.
Return to rem sts and with RS facing, slip centre 28 sts onto a st holder, then rejoin yarn and work in patt to end of row.
Work one row without shaping.
Cast (bind) off 6 sts at beg of next row, then cast (bind) off 5 sts at beg of foll alt row.
Cast (bind) off rem 50 sts.

FRONT

Work Front as for Back.

SLEEVES

Using smaller needles and yarn C, cast on 50 sts.
Work 8cm (3¼") in K1, P1 rib as

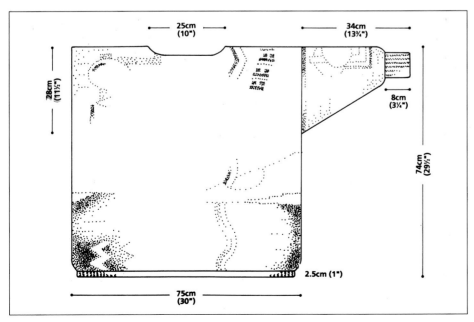

25cm (10")

34cm (13¾")

28cm (11½")

8cm (3¼")

74cm (29½")

2.5cm (1")

75cm (30")

Wonderful colours – and no one would notice if you were careless with your mustard.

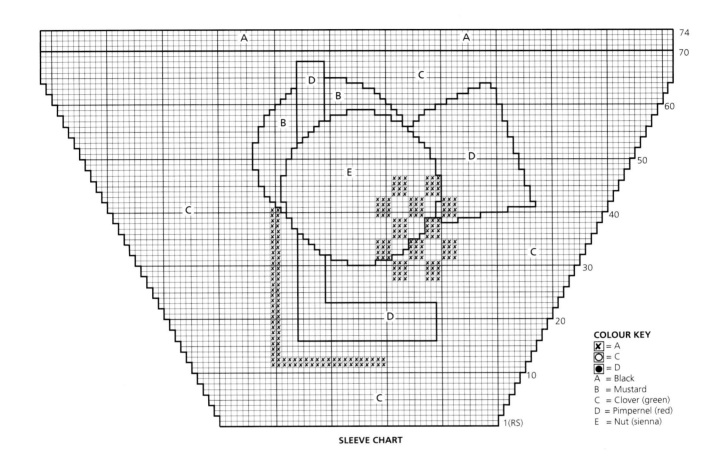

Chart row numbers on right: 74, 70, 60, 50, 40, 30, 20, 10, 1(RS)

COLOUR KEY

☒ = A	
⊙ = C	
◉ = D	

A = Black
B = Mustard
C = Clover (green)
D = Pimpernel (red)
E = Nut (sienna)

SLEEVE CHART

for Back, ending with a WS row.
Change to larger needles and
beg with first chart row (K row),
work in st st foll chart for Sleeve
and at the same time shape
Sleeve by inc one st at each end
of 3rd row and then every foll alt
row until there are 114 sts, so
ending with a RS row.
Cont to foll chart for colour patt
and working in st st throughout,
work without shaping until 74th
chart row has been completed,
so ending with a WS row.
Cast (bind) off all sts.
Make the 2nd Sleeve in the same
way as the first.

NECKBAND
Press pieces lightly on WS with a
warm iron over a damp cloth,
omitting ribbing.
Join right shoulder seam.
Using smaller needles and yarn B

(mustard) and with RS facing,
pick up and K14 sts down left
front neck, K28 sts from front
neck st holder, pick up and K14
sts up right front neck and 14 sts
down right back neck, K28 sts
from back neck st holder and
pick up and K14 sts up left back
neck. 112 sts.
Work in K1, P1 rib for 5cm (2").
Cast (bind) off in rib.

FINISHING
Join left shoulder seam and
neckband.
Placing centre of cast (bound) off
sleeve edge at shoulder seam,
sew Sleeves to Back and Front,
matching sides.
Join the side and the sleeve
seams.
Press seams lightly on WS with a
warm iron over a damp cloth,
omitting ribbing.

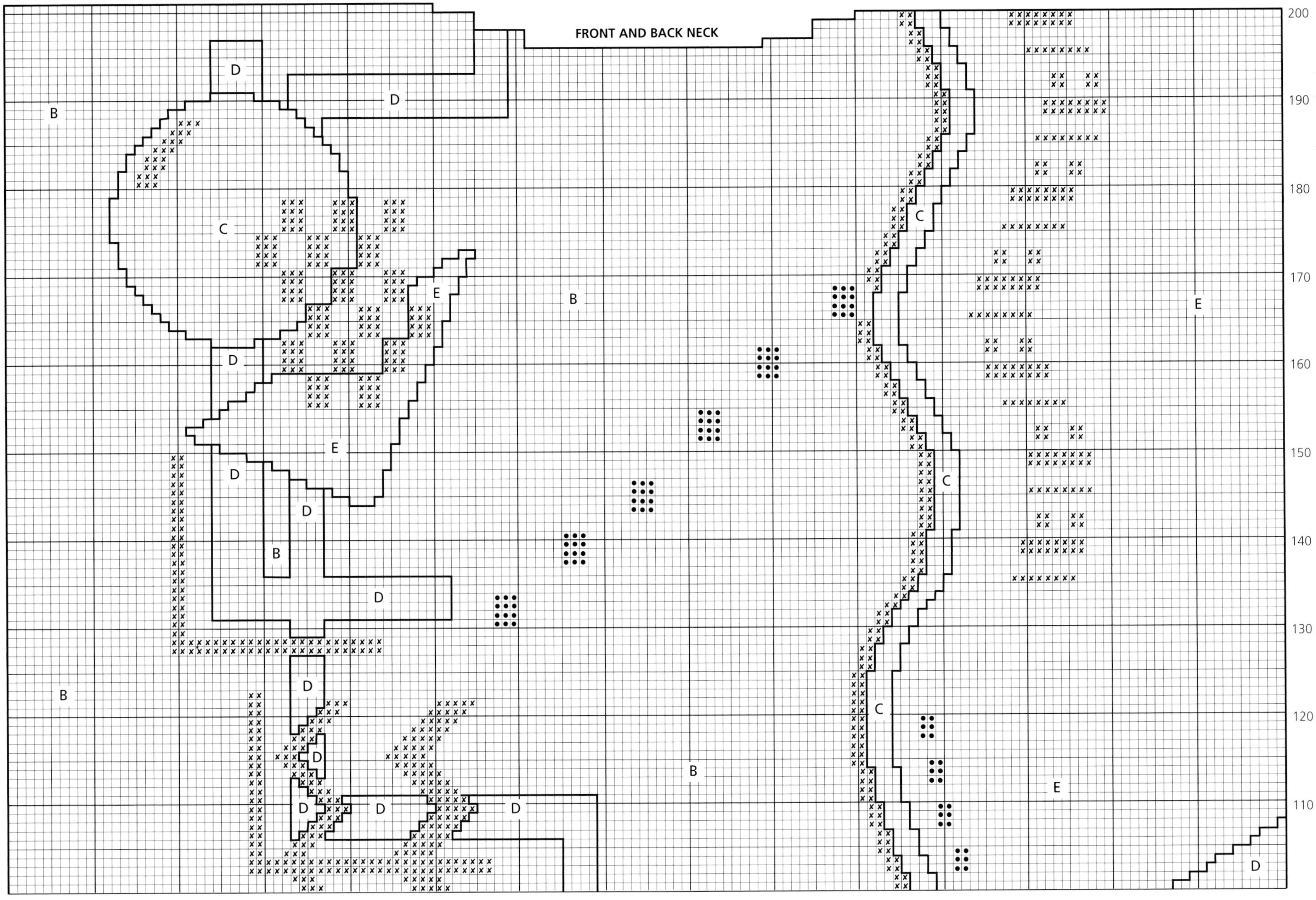
FRONT AND BACK NECK
200
190
180
170
160
150
140
130
120
110
B
C
D
E

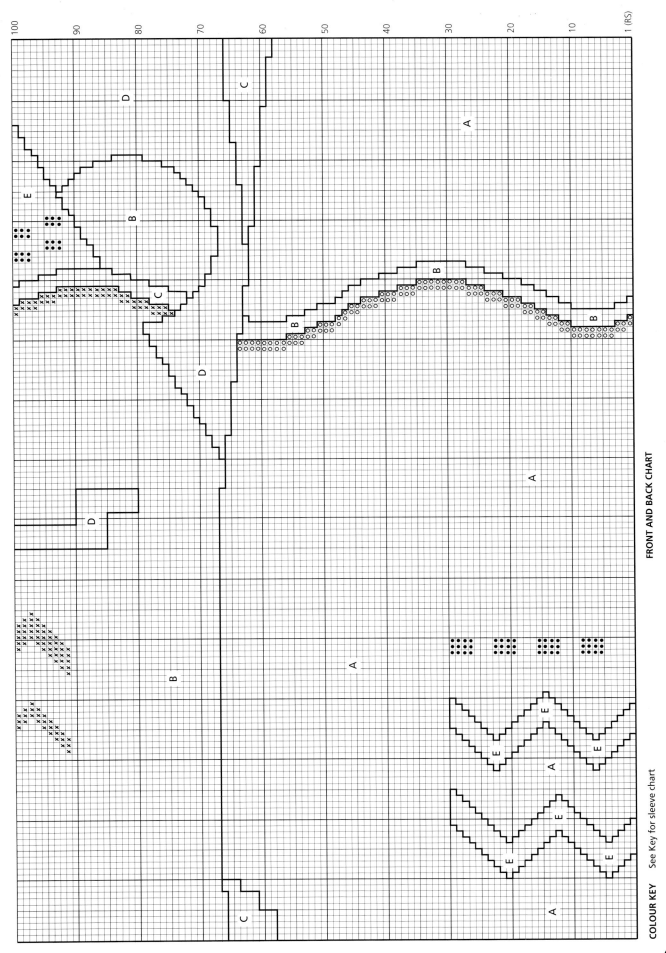

FRONT AND BACK CHART

COLOUR KEY   See Key for sleeve chart

91

WAVES

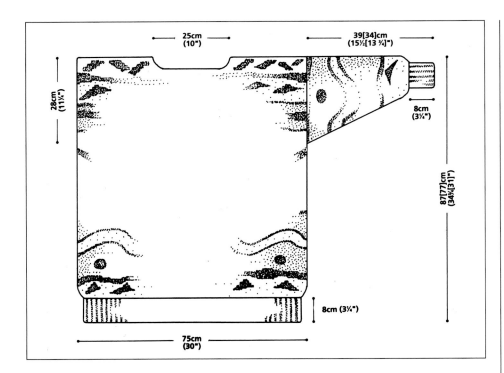

SIZE
One size only, but in two lengths (see page 107 for choosing size)
Finished measurement around bust 150cm (60")

Finished length 87cm (34¾") on longer version and 77cm (31") on shorter version
See diagram for finished measurements of back, front and sleeves (shorter version is in brackets). To lengthen or shorten back and front, or sleeves see page 107.

MATERIALS
Rowan *Handknit DK Cotton*
9 x 50g (1¾oz) balls each in Scarlet (shade no. 255) A and Diana (shade no. 287) B
4 x 50g (1¾oz) balls in Sunflower (shade no. 261) C
6 x 50g (1¾oz) ball in Turkish Plum (shade no. 277) D
One pair each 3¼mm (US size 3) and 4mm (US size 6) needles *or size to obtain correct tension (gauge)*

TENSION (GAUGE)
20 sts and 28 rows to 10cm (4") over st st on 4mm (US size 6) needles
Check your tension (gauge) before beginning.

NOTES
Do not strand yarn across back of work, but use a separate ball or length of yarn for each isolated area of colour, twisting yarns at back when changing colours to avoid holes.
Read charts from right to left for RS (knit) rows and from left to right for WS (purl) rows.

BACK
Using smaller needles and yarn A, cast on 150 sts.
Beg K1, P1 rib as foll:
1st rib row (RS) *K1, P1, rep from * to end.
Rep last row until ribbing measures 8cm (3¼") from beg, ending with a WS row.
Change to larger needles and beg with first chart row (K row) for longer version *or* beg with 27th chart row for shorter version, work in st st foll chart (page 95) for Back (see *Notes* above) until 209th chart row has been completed, so ending with a RS row.
Shape Neck
Cont to foll chart for colour patt and working in st st throughout, beg neck shaping on next row as foll:
210th chart row (WS) P56 sts in patt, turn leaving rem sts on a spare needle.
Working on first side of neck only, dec one st at beg of next row (neck edge) and at neck edge on 3 foll rows, then dec one st at neck edge on 2 foll alt rows. 50 sts.
Work 2 rows without shaping, so ending with 220th chart row.
Cast (bind) off.
Return to rem sts and with WS facing, slip centre 38 sts onto a st holder, then rejoin yarn and P in patt to end of row.
Complete 2nd side of neck to match first side, reversing neck shaping.

FRONT
Work Front as given for Back.

An entire ocean on one jumper!

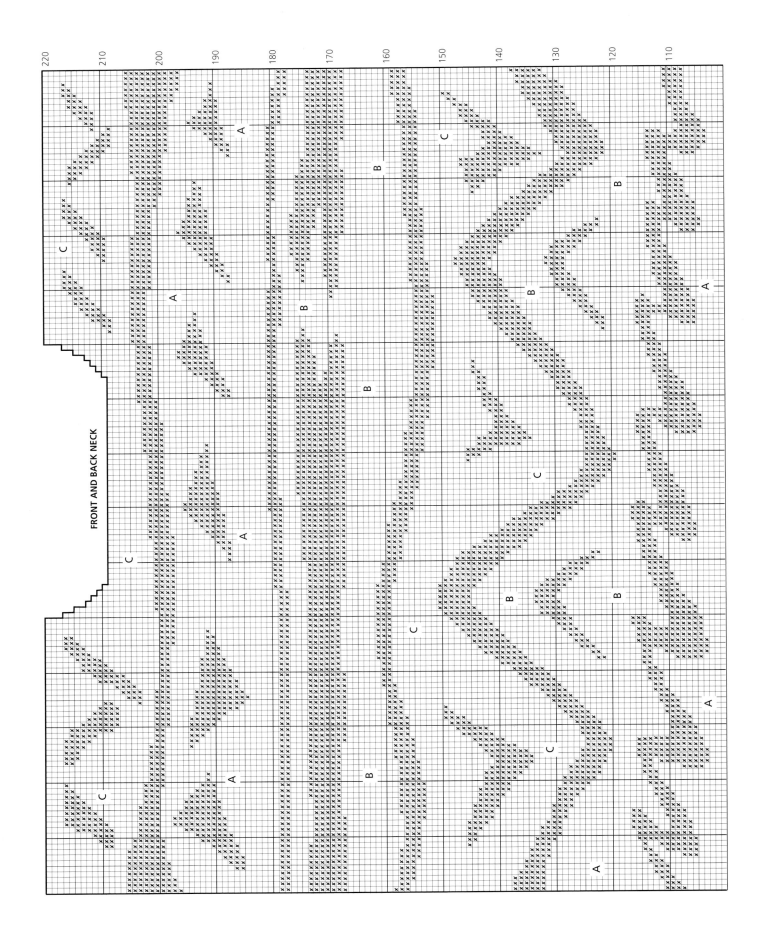

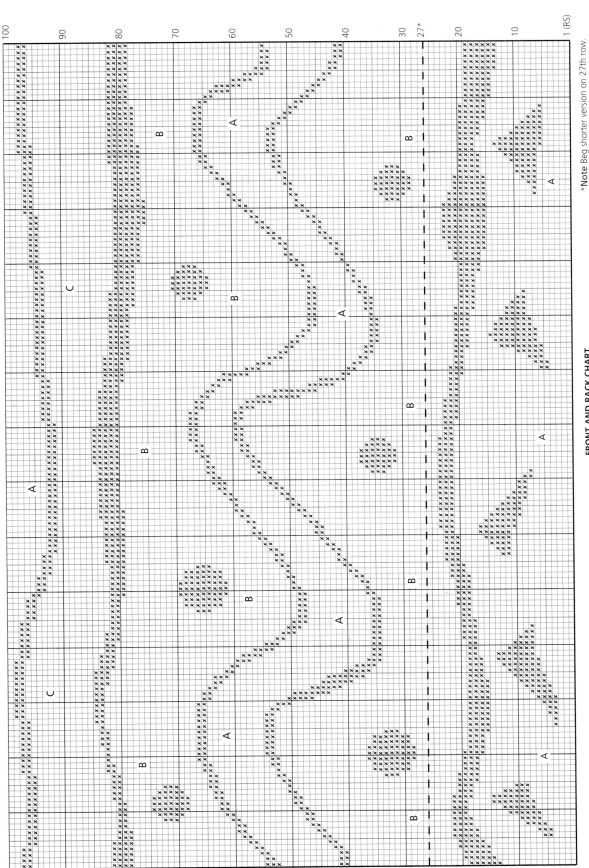

100 90 80 70 60 50 40 30 27* 20 10 1 (RS)

*Note Beg shorter version on 27'th row.

FRONT AND BACK CHART

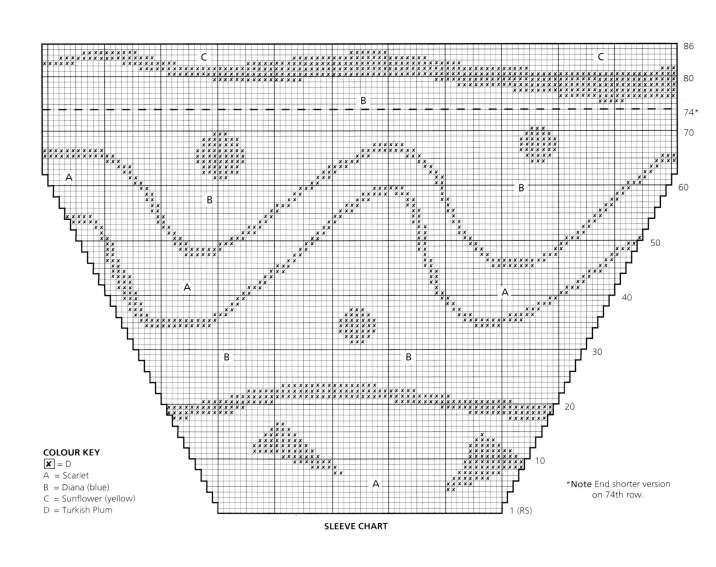

COLOUR KEY
☒ = D
A = Scarlet
B = Diana (blue)
C = Sunflower (yellow)
D = Turkish Plum

SLEEVE CHART

*Note End shorter version on 74th row.

SLEEVES
Using smaller needles and yarn A, cast on 50 sts.
Work 8cm (3¼") in K1, P1 rib as for Back, ending with a WS row.
Change to larger needles and beg with first chart row (K row), work in st st foll chart for Sleeve *and at the same time* shape Sleeve by inc one st at each end of 3rd row and then every foll alt row until there are 112 sts, so ending with a RS row.
Cont to foll chart for colour patt and working in st st throughout, work without shaping until 86th (for longer version) or 74th (for shorter version) chart row has been completed, so ending with a WS row.
Cast (bind) off all sts.
Make the 2nd Sleeve in the same way as the first.

NECKBAND
Press pieces lightly on WS with a warm iron over a damp cloth, omitting ribbing.
Join right shoulder seam.
Using smaller needles and yarn A and with RS facing, pick up and K12 sts down left front neck, K38 sts from front neck st holder, pick up and K12 sts up right front neck and 12 sts down right back neck, K38 sts from back neck st holder and pick up and K12 sts up left back neck. 124 sts.
Work in K1, P1 rib for 5cm (2").
Cast (bind) off in rib.

FINISHING
Join left shoulder seam and neckband. Placing centre of cast (bound) off sleeve edge at shoulder seam, sew Sleeves to Back and Front, matching sides.
Join side and sleeve seams.
Press seams lightly on WS with a warm iron over a damp cloth, omitting ribbing.

MOHAIR JACKET

SIZE

One size only (see page 107 for choosing size)
Finished measurement around bust 180cm (71¾")
See diagram for finished measurements of back, fronts and sleeves. To lengthen or shorten back and fronts, or sleeves see page 107.

MATERIALS

19 x 50g (1¾oz) balls of Patons *Fashion Mohair* in Legend (shade no. 2834)
One pair each 5mm (US size 8) and 5½mm (US size 9) needles *or size to obtain correct tension (gauge)*
Five 2.8cm (1⅛") buttons

TENSION (GAUGE)

15 sts and 20 rows to 10cm (4") over st st on 5½mm (US size 9) needles using yarn A
Check your tension (gauge) before beginning.

BACK

Using smaller needles, cast on 126 sts.
Beg K2, P2 rib as foll:
1st rib row (RS) K2, *P2, K2, rep from * to end.
2nd rib row P2, *K2, P2, rep from * to end.
Rep last 2 rows until ribbing measures 7cm (2¾") from beg, ending with a WS row.
Change to larger needles and beg with a K row, work in st st until Back measures 56cm (21¾") from beg, ending with a WS row.
Shape Armholes
Cont in st st throughout, cast (bind) off 8 sts at beg of next 2 rows. 110 sts.
Work without shaping until Back measures 84cm (33") from beg, ending with a WS row.
Shape Shoulders
Cast (bind) off 13 sts at beg of next 2 rows, then 12 sts at beg of next 4 rows. Cast (bind) off rem 36 sts for back neck.

LEFT FRONT

Using smaller needles, cast on 66 sts.
Work 7cm (2¾") in K2, P2 rib as for Back, ending with a WS row.**
Change to larger needles and beg with a K row, work in st st until there are same number of rows as Back to armhole, ending with a WS row.
Shape Armhole
Cont in st st throughout, cast (bind) off 8 sts at beg of next row (armhole edge). 58 sts.
Work 6 rows without shaping, so ending with a RS row.
Shape V-neck
Keeping armhole edge straight, dec one st at beg of next row (neck edge) and then dec one st at neck edge on every foll alt row until there are 37 sts.
Work without shaping until there are same number of rows as Back to shoulder, ending with a WS row.
Shape Shoulder
Cast (bind) off 13 sts at beg of next row, then cast (bind) off 12 sts at beg of 2 foll alt rows.

RIGHT FRONT

Work as for Left Front to **.
Change to larger needles and beg with a K row, work in st st until there are same number of rows as Back to armhole, ending with a RS row.
Shape Armhole
Cont in st st throughout, cast (bind) off 8 sts at beg of next row (armhole edge). 58 sts.
Work 6 rows without shaping, so ending with a WS row.
Shape V-neck
Keeping armhole edge straight, dec one st at beg of next row (neck edge) and then dec one st at neck edge on every foll alt row until there are 37 sts.
Work without shaping until there are same number of rows as Back to shoulder, ending with a RS row.
Shape Shoulder
Shape shoulder as for Left Front.

SLEEVES

Using smaller needles, cast on 54 sts.
Work 7cm (2¾") in K2, P2 rib as for Back, ending with a WS row.

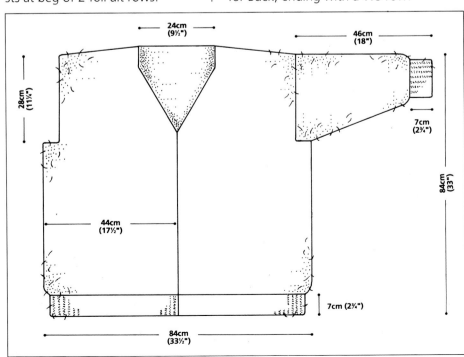

It's fluffy, it's purple – it's utterly fab.

Change to larger needles and beg with a K row, work in st st, inc one st at each end of 3rd row and every foll alt row until there are 84 sts.

Work in st st without shaping until Sleeve measures 46cm (18") from beg or desired length, ending with a WS row.

Cast (bind) off all sts.

Make the 2nd Sleeve in the same way as the first.

BUTTON BAND AND COLLAR

Join shoulder seams.

Using smaller needles, cast on 18 sts.

Beg K1, P1 rib as foll:

1st rib row (K1, P1) 9 times.

Rep last row until Band, when slightly stretched, fits up Left Front from cast-on edge to beg of neck shaping.

Shape Collar

Beg shaping Collar on next row as foll:

***Next row** K1, P1, (K1, P1, K1) all into next st, P1, *K1, P1, rep from * to end.

Work 3 rows in rib without shaping.***

Rep from *** to *** 14 times more (incs are always at outer edge of Collar). 48 sts.

Cont in rib without shaping until Collar fits up Left Front neck edge to centre back neck.

Cast (bind) off loosely in rib.

Sew Button Band and Collar to centre front edge of Left Front (with incs at outer edge of Collar), ending at centre back neck.

Mark positions for 5 buttons on Button Band, the first 5cm (2") from cast-on edge, the top one at beg of V-neck shaping, and the 3 others evenly spaced between.

BUTTONHOLE BAND AND COLLAR

Work as for Button Band and Collar, making buttonholes to correspond with the markers as foll:

1st buttonhole row Rib 7, cast (bind) off 4 sts, rib to end.

2nd buttonhole row Rib 7, cast on 4 sts, rib 7.

POCKETS

Place 2 markers on right armhole edge of Back, the first 20cm (8") below armhole shaping and the 2nd 35cm (13¼") below armhole shaping.

Using larger needles and with RS facing, pick up and K24 sts between markers.

Beg with a P row, work 7 rows in st st, so ending with a P row.

Shape Pocket

Beg shaping Pocket on next row as foll:

Next row (RS) K into front and back of first 2 sts, K to end. 26 sts.

Cont in st st throughout, cast (bind) off 2 sts at beg of next row (top edge of pocket) and at beg of every foll alt row until 2 sts rem.

Cast (bind) off 2 rem sts.

Work 3 more pocket pieces in the same way, one on the left armhole edge of the Back, one on the Left Front and one on the Right Front, reversing shaping where necessary.

FINISHING

Placing centre of cast (bound) off sleeve edge at shoulder seam, sew cast (bound) off edge of Sleeves to vertical edge of armholes and sew cast (bound) off edge of armhole to sides of Sleeves.

Working a flat seam, join side and sleeve seams, sewing around pockets on side seams when reached.

Sew Buttonhole Band and Collar to centre front edge of Right Front (with incs at outer edge of Collar), ending at centre back neck. Join centre back collar seam.

Sew on buttons to correspond to buttonholes.

Press seams lightly on WS, following instructions on yarn label and omitting ribbing.

AUTUMN JACKET

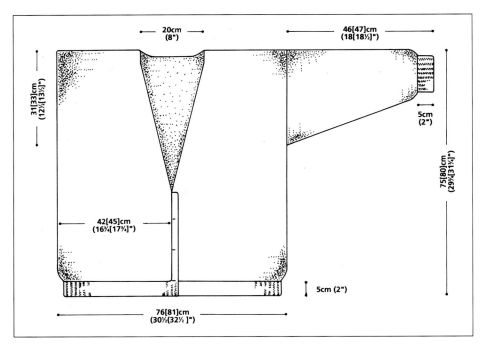

SIZES

To choose appropriate size see page 107
Finished measurement around bust 160[171]cm (64[68]")
Figures for larger size are given in brackets []; where there is only one set of figures, it applies to both sizes.
See diagram for finished measurements of back, fronts and sleeves. To lengthen or shorten back and fronts, or sleeves see page 107.

MATERIALS

14[15] x 100g (3½oz) hanks of Rowan *Chunky Fox Tweed* in main colour — Moorland (shade no. 871) A
2 x 100g (3½oz) hanks of Rowan *Chunky Cotton Chenille* in Black (shade no. 367) B for collar
One pair each 4mm (US size 6), 4½mm (US size 7) and 5½mm (US size 9) needles *or size to obtain correct tension (gauge)*
Three 2.8cm (1⅛") buttons

TENSION (GAUGE)

15 sts and 22 rows to 10cm (4") over st st on 5½mm (US size 9) needles using yarn A
Check your tension (gauge) before beginning.

BACK

Using 4mm (US size 6) needles and yarn A, cast on 112[120] sts.
Beg K1, P1 rib as foll:
1st rib row (RS) *K1, P1, rep from * to end.
Rep last row until ribbing measures 5cm (2") from beg, ending with a WS row and inc one st at each end of last row. 114[122] sts.
Change to 5½mm (US size 9) needles and beg with a K row, work in st st until Back measures 75[80]cm (29¾[31¾]") from beg, ending with a WS row.
Shape Neck
Beg neck shaping on next row as foll:
Next row (RS) K48[52] and slip these sts onto a st holder for right back neck, cast (bind) off next 18 sts, K to end.
Working on left side of neck only, P one row.
Cont in st st throughout, cast (bind) off 6 sts at beg of next row (neck edge).

Work one row without shaping.
Cast (bind) off rem 42[46] sts.
Return to rem sts and with WS facing, rejoin yarn A and cast (bind) off 6 sts, then P to end of row.
Work 2 rows without shaping.
Cast (bind) off rem 42[46] sts.

LEFT FRONT

Using 4mm (US size 6) needles and yarn A, cast on 68[72] sts.
Work 5cm (2") in K1, P1 rib as for Back, ending with a WS row and inc one st at end of last row. 69[73] sts.**
Change to 5½mm (US size 9) needles and work next row as foll:
Next row (RS) K to last 6 sts, *P1, K1*, rep from * to * twice more.
Next row *P1, K1*, rep from * to * twice more, P to end.
Rep last 2 rows until Left Front measures 29[34]cm (11½[13½]") from beg, ending with a WS row.
Shape V-neck
Beg V-neck shaping on next row as foll:
Next row (RS) K to last 6 (rib) sts, slip these 6 sts onto a st holder to be used later for Collar. 63[67] sts.
Cont in st st throughout, dec one st at beg of next row (neck edge) and then at neck edge on every foll 4th row until there are 42[46] sts.
Work without shaping until there are same number of rows as Back to shoulder.
Cast (bind) off.
Mark positions for 3 buttons on Button Band (6 rib sts at centre front edge), the first to come on the first row of st st, the top one 9cm (3½") below beg of neck shaping and the 3rd one evenly spaced between.

RIGHT FRONT

Work as for Left Front to **.
Change to 5½mm (US size 9) knitting needles and work next row as foll:

1st buttonhole row (RS) K1, P1, K1, cast (bind) off next 3 sts in rib, K to end.
2nd buttonhole row P to last 6 sts, cast on 3 sts, P1, K1, P1.
Next row *K1, P1*, rep from * to * twice more, K to end.
Next row P to last 6 sts, *K1, P1*, rep from * to * twice more.
Rep last 2 rows until Right Front measures same as Left Front to beg of neck shaping *and at the same* time work 2 more buttonholes in the same way to correspond with markers, ending with a RS row.

Shape V-neck
Beg V-neck shaping on next row as foll:
Next row (WS) P to last 6 (rib) sts, slip these 6 sts onto a st holder to be used later for Collar. 63[67] sts.
Cont in st st throughout, dec one st at beg of next row (neck edge) and then at neck edge on every foll 4th row until there are 42[46] sts.
Work without shaping until there are same number of rows as Back to shoulder. Cast (bind) off.

SLEEVES
Using 4mm (US size 6) needles and yarn A, cast on 55[59] sts.
Beg K1, P1 rib as foll:
1st rib row (RS) K1, *P1, K1, rep from * to end.
2nd rib row P1, *K1, P1, rep from * to end.
Rep last 2 rows until ribbing measures 5cm (2") from beg, ending with a WS row.
Change to 5½mm (US size 9) needles and beg with a K row, work in st st, inc one st at each end of 3rd row and every foll 3rd row until there are 95[101] sts.
Work in st st without shaping until Sleeve measures 46[47]cm (18[18½]") from beg or desired length, ending with a WS row.
Cast (bind) off all sts.
Make the 2nd Sleeve in the same way as the first.

COLLAR
Press pieces lightly on WS with a warm iron over a damp cloth, omitting ribbing.
Join shoulder seams.
Using 4½mm (US size 7) needles and yarn B and with WS facing, work K1, P1 rib across 6 sts on st holder on Right Front as foll:
1st rib row (WS) (K1, P1) twice, K into front and back of next st, K1 (so ending at outer edge of Collar).
2nd rib row Sl 1 knitwise, (K1, P1) 3 times.
Keeping K1, P1 rib correct as set throughout, cont as foll:
3rd rib row Rib to last 2 sts, work into front and back of next st, K1.
4th rib row Sl 1 knitwise, rib to end.
Rep 3rd and 4th rib rows (so inc one st on every alt row at outside edge of Collar) until there are 68 sts.
Mark each end of last inc row with a contrasting thread.
Work without shaping until Collar, when slightly stretched, fits up neck edge of Left Front to centre back neck.

Mark each end of last row with a contrasting thread.
Now working Collar in reverse for other side of neck, cont in rib without shaping until length from centre back neck matches length between 2 sets of markers, ending at inner edge of Collar.
Then beg decreasing on next row as foll:
Next row Rib to last 3 sts, work next 2 sts tog, K1 (so ending at outer edge of Collar).
Next row Sl 1 knitwise, rib to end.
Rep last 2 rows until there are 6 sts.
Graft these 6 sts onto 6 sts on st holder on Left Front.

FINISHING
Sew Collar to neck edge.
Placing centre of cast (bound) off sleeve edge at shoulder seam, sew Sleeves to Back and Fronts, matching sides.
Join side and sleeve seams.
Sew on buttons to correspond to buttonholes.
Press seams lightly on WS, following instructions on yarn label and omitting ribbing.

CHENILLE JACKET

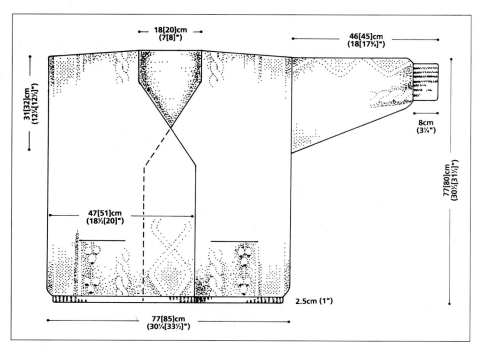

SIZES
To choose appropriate size see page 107
Finished measurement around bust 154[170]cm (60½[67]")
Figures for larger size are given in brackets []; where there is only one set of figures, it applies to both sizes.
See diagram for finished measurements of back, fronts and sleeves. To lengthen or shorten back and fronts, or sleeves see page 107.

MATERIALS
11 [13] x 100g (3½oz) hanks of Rowan *Chunky Cotton Chenille* in Chestnut (shade no. 373)
One pair each 5mm (US size 8) and 6mm (US size 10) needles *or size to obtain correct tension (gauge)*
Cable needle (cn)
10 stitch markers (see *Notes*)

TENSION (GAUGE)
13 sts and 22 rows to 10cm (4") over st st on 6mm (US size 10) needles
Check your tension (gauge) before beginning.

NOTES
Several st patts are worked in panels across the Back, Fronts and Sleeves. The charts provided indicate the number of sts across the first row of each st patt panel.
Instructions are given for placing st markers between the panels. These st markers are slipped in each row so that they are always positioned on the needles between the panels as a guide for the knitter. An experienced knitter may not find the st markers necessary, but it is still advisable to use markers on each side of the knotted rope panels as the number of sts in this patt varies.

KNOTTED ROPE PANEL
This panel is begun over 3 sts, but sts are increased and decreased over the 24-row patt rep so that the number of sts across panel varies.
1st row (RS) P1, K1, P1.
2nd row and all WS rows K all K sts and P all P sts.
3rd row As first row.
5th row As first row.

7th row P1, K into the front, back and front of next st, P1. (5 sts)
9th row P1, K3, P1.
11th row P1, K3tog, P1. (3 sts)
13th row K into front, back and front of first st, P1, K into front, back and front of next st. (7 sts)
15th row K3, P1, K3.
17th row K3tog, P1, K3tog. (3 sts)
19th, 21st and 23rd rows As first row.
24th row As 2nd row.
These 24 rows are repeated to form the knotted rope patt.

CABLE PANEL
This panel is worked over 22 sts for the Back and Fronts.
The cable panel on the Sleeves is worked over 16 sts (see the Sleeve instructions for the alteration).
1st row (RS) P8, K6, P8.
2nd row K8, P6, K8.
3rd and 4th rows As first and 2nd rows.
5th row P8, slip next 3 sts onto a cable needle (cn) and hold at front of work, K next 3 sts from LH needle, then K3 from cn, P8.
6th row As 2nd row.
7th and 8th rows As first and 2nd rows.
These 8 rows are repeated to form the cable patt.

LOZENGE PANEL
This panel is worked over 21 sts.
1st row (RS) P6, slip next st onto a cn and hold at back of work, K next 3 sts from LH needle, then K1 from cn — called *cable 4 right* or *C4R* —, P1, slip next 3 sts onto a cn and hold at front of work, K next st from LH needle, then K3 from cn — called *cable 4 left* or *C4L* —, P6.
2nd row K6, P4, K1, P4, K6.
3rd row P5, C4R, P1, K1, P1, C4L, P5.
4th row K5, P4, K1, P1, K1, P4, K5.
5th row P4, C4R, P1, (K1, P1) twice, C4L, P4.

The kind of woolly the devil would wear – hot stuff! (Hole in the back for forked tail optional.)

6th row K4, P4, K1, (P1, K1) twice, P4, K4.
7th row P3, C4R, P1, (K1, P1) 3 times, C4L, P3.
8th row K3, P4, K1, (P1, K1) 3 times, P4, K3.
9th row P2, C4R, P1, (K1, P1) 4 times, C4L, P2.
10th row K2, P4, K1, (P1, K1) 4 times, P4, K2.
11th row P1, C4R, P1, (K1, P1) 5 times, C4L, P1.
12th row K1, P4, K1, (P1, K1) 5 times, P4, K1.
13th row C4R, P1, (K1, P1) 6 times, C4L.
14th row P4, K1, (P1, K1) 6 times, P4.
15th row K3, P1, (K1, P1) 7 times, K3.
16th row P3, K1, (P1, K1) 7 times, P3.
17th row Slip next 3 sts onto a cn and hold at front of work, P next st from LH needle, then K3 sts from cn — called *twist 4 left* or *T4L* —, P1, (K1, P1) 6 times, slip next st onto a cn and hold at back of work, K next 3 sts from LH needle, then P1 from cn — called *twist 4 right* or *T4R*.
18th row K1, P3, K1, (P1, K1) 6 times, P3, K1.
19th row P1, T4L, P1, (K1, P1) 5 times, T4R, P1.
20th row K2, P3, K1, (P1, K1) 5 times, P3, K2.
21st row P2, T4L, P1, (K1, P1) 4 times, T4R, P2.
22nd row K3, P3, K1, (P1, K1) 4 times, P3, K3.
23rd row P3, T4L, P1, (K1, P1) 3 times, T4R, P3.
24th row K4, P3, K1, (P1, K1) 3 times, P3, K4.
25th row P4, T4L, P1, (K1, P1) twice, T4R, P4.
26th row K5, P3, K1, (P1, K1) twice, P3, K5.
27th row P5, T4L, P1, K1, P1, T4R, P5.
28th row K6, P3, K1, P1, K1, P3, K6.
29th row P6, T4L, P1, T4R, P6.
30th row K7, P3, K1, P3, K7.
31st row P7, slip next 4 sts onto

a cn and hold at back of work, K next 3 sts from LH needle, then K4 sts from cn — called *cable 7 back* or *C7B* —, P7.
32nd row K7, P7, K7.
These 32 rows are repeated to form the lozenge patt.

BACK
Using smaller needles, cast on 105[115] sts.
Beg K1, P1 rib as foll:
1st rib row (RS) P1, *K1, P1, rep from * to end.
2nd rib row K1, *P1, K1, rep from * to end.
Rep last 2 rows until ribbing measures 2.5cm (1") from beg, ending with a WS row and inc 4 sts evenly across last row. 109[119] sts.
Change to larger needles and position patt sts across Back (see *Notes* above) as foll:
1st patt row (RS) P5[6] and slip st marker onto RH needle; (K1, P1) 4[6] times and slip st marker onto RH needle; P2, K2, P2 and slip st marker onto RH needle; work first row of knotted rope panel over next 3 sts and slip on st marker; work first row of cable panel over next 22 sts and slip on st marker; work first row of lozenge panel over next 21 sts and slip on st marker; work first row of cable panel over next 22 sts and slip on st marker; work first row of knotted rope panel over next 3 sts and slip on st marker; P2, K2, P2 and slip on st marker; (K1, P1) 4[6] times and slip on marker; P5[6].
2nd patt row K5[6] and slip marker; (P1, K1) 4[6] times and slip marker; K2, P2, K2 and slip marker; work 2nd row of knotted rope panel over next 3 sts and slip marker; work 2nd row of cable panel over next 22 sts and slip marker; work 2nd row of lozenge panel over next 21 sts and slip marker; work 2nd row of cable panel over next 22 sts and slip marker; work 2nd row of knotted rope panel over next 3

sts and slip marker; K2, P2, K2 and slip marker; (P1, K1) 4[6] times and slip marker; K5[6].
Cont in patt as set (working knotted rope, cable and lozenge panels between markers foll row by row instructions, and working rem sts as set in first and 2nd patt rows above) until Back measures 77[80]cm (30½[31½]") from beg, ending with a WS row.
Shape Shoulders
Keeping patt correct throughout and casting (binding) off in patt, cast (bind) off 14[16] sts at beg of next 2 rows, then 14[15] sts at beg of next 4 rows.
Cast (bind) off rem 25[27] sts in patt for back neck.

LEFT FRONT
Before beg Left Front, make pocket lining.
Pocket Lining
Using larger needles, cast on 22 sts.
Work in rev st st until lining measures 20cm (8") from beg, ending with a WS (K) row.
Break off yarn and slip sts onto a st holder to be used later.
Begin Left Front
Using smaller needles, cast on 59[63] sts.
Work 2.5cm (1") in K1, P1 rib as for Back, ending with a WS row and inc 8[9] sts evenly across last row. 67[72] sts.**
Change to larger needles and position patt sts across Left Front as foll:
1st patt row (RS) P5[6] and slip st marker onto RH needle; (K1, P1) 4[6] times and slip st marker onto RH needle; P2, K2, P2 and slip st marker onto RH needle; work first row of knotted rope panel over next 3 sts and slip on st marker; work first row of cable panel over next 22 sts and slip on st marker; work first row of lozenge panel over next 21 sts and slip on st marker; P2.
2nd patt row K2 and slip marker; work 2nd row of lozenge panel over next 21 sts and slip

marker; work 2nd row of cable panel over next 22 sts and slip marker; work 2nd row of knotted rope panel over next 3 sts and slip marker; K2, P2, K2 and slip marker; (P1, K1) 4[6] times and slip marker; K5[6].

Cont in patt as set until Left Front measures 23cm (9") from beg, ending with a WS row (and ending with a row which has only 3 sts across the knotted rope panel).

Place Pocket

Keeping patt correct as set throughout, place pocket on next row as foll:

Next row (RS) Work 14[19] sts in patt, slip next 22 sts onto a st holder, then with RS facing, work the 22 sts of the pocket lining from the st holder in patt, work in patt to end.

Work without shaping until Left Front measures 41[44]cm (16[17¼]") from beg, ending with a RS row.

Shape V-neck

Dec one st at beg of next row (neck edge) and at neck edge on every foll alt row 25[26] times in all. 42[46] sts rem (counting knotted rope panel as 3 sts only). Work without shaping until there are same number of rows as Back to shoulder, ending with a WS row.

Shape Shoulder

Cast (bind) off 14[16] sts at beg of next row, then cast (bind) off 14[15] sts at beg of 2 foll alt rows.

RIGHT FRONT

Work as for Left Front to **.
Change to larger needles and position patt sts across Right Front as foll:

1st patt row (RS) P2 and slip st marker onto RH needle; work first row of lozenge panel over next 21 sts and slip on st marker; work first row of cable panel over next 22 sts and slip on st marker; work first row of knotted rope panel over next 3 sts and slip on

st marker; P2, K2, P2 and slip on st marker; (K1, P1) 4[6] times and slip on marker; P5[6].

2nd patt row K5[6] and slip marker; (P1, K1) 4[6] times and slip marker; K2, P2, K2 and slip marker; work 2nd row of knotted rope panel over next 3 sts and slip marker; work 2nd row of cable panel over next 22 sts and slip marker; work 2nd row of lozenge panel over next 21 sts and slip marker; K2.

Cont in patt as set until there are same number of rows as Left Front to pocket, so ending with a WS row.

Place Pocket

Keeping patt correct as set throughout, place pocket on next row as foll:

Next row (RS) Work 31 sts in patt, slip next 22 sts onto a st holder, then with RS facing, work the 22 sts of the pocket lining from the st holder in patt, work in patt to end.

Work without shaping until Right Front measures same as Left Front to neck shaping, ending with a WS row.

Shape V-neck

Dec one st at beg of next row (neck edge) and at neck edge on every foll alt row 25[26] times in all. 42[46] sts rem (counting knotted rope panel as 3 sts only). Work without shaping until there are same number of rows as Back to shoulder, ending with a RS row.

Shape Shoulder

Shape shoulder as for Left Front.

SLEEVES

Using smaller needles, cast on 45[47] sts.

Work 8cm (3¼") in K1, P1 rib as for Back, ending with a WS row and inc 10[12] sts evenly across last row. 55[59] sts.

Change to larger needles and position patt sts across Sleeve as foll:

1st patt row (RS) K0[1], P0[1], K1 and slip st marker onto RH

needle; P2, K6, P8 for first row of cable panel over next 16 sts and slip on st marker; work first row of lozenge panel over next 21 sts and slip on st marker; P8, K6, P2 for first row of cable panel over next 16 sts and slip on st marker; K1, P0[1], K0[1].

2nd patt row K0[1], P0[1], K1 and slip marker; K2, P6, K8 for 2nd row of cable panel over next

STITCH PATTERNS ACROSS CHENILLE JACKET BACK

rev st st	moss (seed) st	P2,K2,P2 (RS)	knotted rope	cable panel	lozenge panel	cable panel	knotted rope	P2,K2,P2 (RS)	moss (seed) st	rev st st	
5[6]	8[12]	6	3*	22	21	22	3*	6	8[12]	5[6]	sts

STITCH PATTERNS ACROSS CHENILLE JACKET LEFT FRONT

rev st st	lozenge panel	cable panel	knotted rope	P2,K2,P2 (RS)	moss (seed) st	rev st st	
2	21	22	3*	6	8[12]	5[6]	sts

STITCH PATTERNS ACROSS CHENILLE JACKET RIGHT FRONT

rev st st	moss (seed) st	P2,K2,P2 (RS)	knotted rope	cable panel	lozenge panel	rev st st	
5[6]	8[12]	6	3*	22	21	2	sts

STITCH PATTERNS ACROSS CHENILLE JACKET SLEEVES

moss (seed) st	cable panel	lozenge panel	cable panel	moss (seed) st	
1[3]	16	21	16	1[3]	sts

*__Note__ *The number of sts across the knotted rope st patt vary, but there are 3 sts in the first patt row.*

16 sts and slip marker; work 2nd row of lozenge panel over next 21 sts and slip marker; K8, P6, K2 for first row of cable panel over next 16 sts and slip st marker; K1, P0[1], K0[1].
(*Note:* The cable panel is worked over 16 sts instead of 22 sts and the position of the 6 cable sts has been set in the first 2 patt rows above.)
Cont in patt as set, inc one st at each end of next row and every foll 3rd row until there are 89[91] sts *and at the same time* work all extra sts outside first and last st markers in moss (seed) st.
Work in patt without shaping until Sleeve measures 46[45]cm (18[17¾]") from beg or desired length, ending with a WS row.
Cast (bind) off all sts in patt.

Make the 2nd Sleeve in the same way as the first.

COLLAR
Do not press.
Join shoulder seams.
Using smaller needles, cast on 14 sts.
Work in moss (seed) st until Collar, when slightly stretched, fits up centre edge of Right Front from cast-on edge to neck shaping. Keeping moss (seed) st correct throughout, inc one st at beg of next row and at same edge on every foll 4th row until there are 28 sts.
Work without shaping until Collar reaches centre back neck.
Cast (bind) off in patt.
Work the 2nd half of the Collar in exactly the same way.

FINISHING
Sew the Collar pieces to Fronts, with increased edges of Collar to neck edges. Join collar seam at centre back neck.
Pocket Top
Using smaller needles and with RS of Left Front facing, work in K1, P1 rib across 22 sts from st holder at pocket top.
Work 2.5cm (1") in K1, P1 rib.
Cast (bind) off in rib.
Work pocket top on Right Front in the same way.
Sew pocket linings neatly to WS of Fronts. Sew ends of pocket tops to RS.
Placing centre of cast (bound) off sleeve edge at shoulder seam, sew Sleeves to Back and Fronts, matching sides.
Join side and sleeve seams.

KNITTING TECHNIQUES

HOW TO CHOOSE YOUR SIZE

Each design in this book is accompanied by a diagram giving the actual finished measurements. Using the diagrams you can choose which garment to knit depending on the desired looseness rather than on a specific size that is supposed to 'fit' your particular measurements. Many of the designs are one size only, but where alternative sizes are given, you have a choice between a loose-fitting or a more close-fitting look.

Obviously, the greater the difference between the actual finished measurement and your bust measurement the looser the garment will be. If in doubt as to what type of fit your prefer, measure a favourite sweater to use as a guideline.

There is very little shaping on any of the designs in order that someone with a bust measurement of 92cm (36"), for example, can wear the same garment as someone with a 127cm (50") bust. The sweater would obviously look different on different wearers, but the style remains the same.

HOW TO ADJUST YOUR GARMENT

Although the garments included will fit a wide range of sizes, you may still wish to alter sleeve or body lengths, or even the body width in some instances.

Adjusting Sleeve Length

Sleeve length is a vital measurement and may be the only one needing adjustment if there are any adjustments at all to be made.

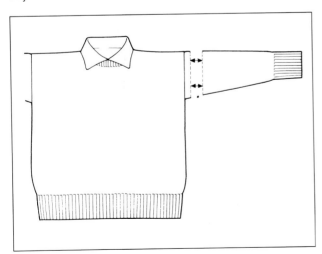

To make a sleeve longer (above), just work the extra rows *after* the sleeve shaping has been completed at the top of the sleeve. To shorten the length decrease the number of rows, making sure that the correct number of stitches has been increased first.

Most sleeve designs have a section which is worked straight (without shaping) at the top of the sleeve so that there is room for shortening. If,

however, you wish to shorten more than has been allowed for in the instructions you may have to work the increases closer together. For instance, if the pattern calls for increasing one stitch at each end of every 4th row, this may be altered to increasing at each end of every 3rd row until the correct number of stitches has been increased.

Adjusting Body Length

The method for adjusting the body length of your garment depends on the specific design.

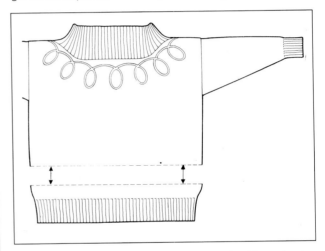

To alter length of a plain garment worked in a single colour (above), simply add or subtract the required number of centimetres (inches).

If the length is calculated by the number of rows instead of centimetres (inches) use the row tension (gauge) to work out the adjustment. For example, if you wish to lengthen by 5cm (2") and you are working to a tension (gauge) of 28 rows to 10cm (4") then add 14 rows. Always remember to make the body length alteration before the armhole shaping and before the neck shaping.

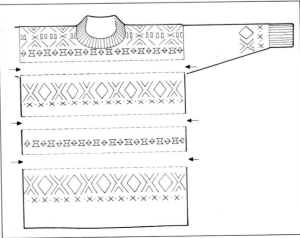

Changing lengths on a design which has a colourwork pattern must be done very carefully so as not to alter the charted motifs. Therefore, the alteration should be made either before the chart is begun or between the motifs (see previous page).

Adjusting Body Width

To adjust the width of your garment, once you have decided how much you need to add or subtract, refer to the tension (gauge) to work out how many stitches this will involve. If, for example, you wish to remove 5cm (2") from the width of the back and front and the tension (gauge) is 24 stiches to 10cm (4") then subtract 12 stitches.

The most important thing to remember is that after adding or subtracting stitches on a garment which later becomes shaped – the neck for instance – allow for the addition or subtraction of these stitches when following subsequent instructions.

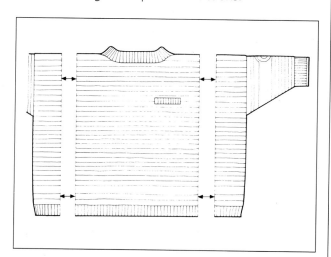

The loss or gain of stitches should be placed evenly on either side of the neck shaping so as not to alter the neck size (above). Also, remember that after changing the body width the sleeve length may need to be adjusted to compensate.

Again care must be taken when adjusting width on a design that follows a colourwork chart and it is not advised for an inexperienced knitter to attempt doing this.

TENSION (GAUGE)

The golden rule for knitters is – 'always check your tension'. Before starting any garment you should make a tension (gauge) sample in order to measure your tension (gauge) against that given in the pattern instructions. Failing to make a tension (gauge) sample may mean that the measurements of your finished garment will turn out to be very different from the measurements given in the instructions, thereby spoiling the appearance of the garment.

Make a tension (gauge) sample by using the yarn, needles and stitch pattern specified under 'Tension (Gauge)'. Knit the sample slightly larger than 10cm (4") square.

Smooth out the finished sample on a flat surface being careful not to stretch it. Using pins, mark out the number of stiches and rows given in the instructions for 10cm (4"). If the specified number of stitches knit up wider than 10cm (4"), then your knitting is too loose and you should change your needles to a smaller size. If they knit up narrower than 10cm (4"), then your knitting is too tight and you should change your needles to a larger size.

STRANDING YARN

One method used when knitting with more than one colour across a row is stranding the yarns on the wrong side of the knitted fabric.

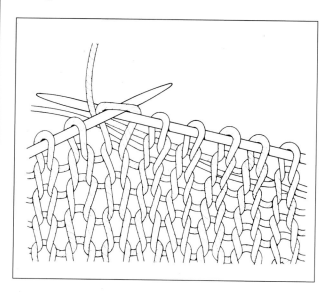

On a knit row, always keeping the contrasting colours at the back of the work, knit the required number of stitches with the first colour. Then drop the first colour and work with the 2nd colour as required, and so on.

The yarns should be stranded loosely across the back, but not so loosely that that they form any suggestion of a loop. Strand in the same way on a purl row, always keeping the contrasting colours at the front of the work.

When using this method of colour knitting, strand yarn only over two to five stitches. If the yarn needs to be stranded over longer distances weave the yarn over and under the working yarn after every three or four stitches. Only use the stranding method if it is called for in the knitting instructions.

INTARSIA KNITTING

The other method used for colour knitting is called *intarsia*. In intarsia knitting the contrasting colours are only worked in isolated areas and are not stranded across the entire row. The knitting instructions will indicate when the motifs should be worked with separate balls of yarn in isolated areas.

When working in intarsia every time the colour is changed the yarns are twisted together to avoid creating a hole in the knitted fabric. A good example of this type of knitting is seen in the *Jazz* sweater (see page 57), where it is obvious that it is not necessary to carry a particular colour past where it is needed in a row.

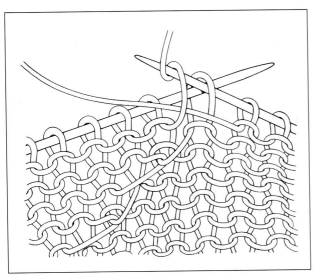

As with stranded knitting, the contrasting colours are always dropped to the wrong side of the knitting. The yarns are twisted together by crossing them before picking up the new colour (see above).

FINISHING

Good finishing (described below) makes all the difference to the final success of your knitted garment.

Darning in Loose Ends

Loose ends on the wrong side of your knitting look untidy and if left loose are in danger of coming through to the right side and creating holes. While knitting when beginning a new yarn always leave long enough loose ends to finish off later.

To darn in loose ends after your garment pieces are completed, thread each end in turn into a blunt-pointed tapestry needle and weave it into the back of the knitting. The ends can then be safely trimmed close to the fabric. When working with different coloured yarns, darn the ends into the same coloured stitches for a neat effect.

Blocking and Pressing

Before pattern pieces are sewn together, they are usually blocked and pressed to ensure a good fit. It is always a best to check the yarn label for any special pressing instructions before beginning any blocking.

To prepare a padded surface for blocking lay a folded blanket on a table and cover it with a sheet. Place the knitted pieces wrong side up on top of the sheet, smoothing them out to the correct measurements. Being careful not to stretch or distort the fabric and making sure that all rows run in straight lines, pin the pieces in position using rustproof pins.

Then using a warm iron and a damp cloth, lay the iron gently on the fabric. Do not move the iron over the surface, but lift it up each time before moving it on. Remove the pins only after the knitting has cooled and dried completely. Do not press ribbing and use care when pressing raised patterns, such as the pattern on the *Aran Jacket* (page 22).

Edge to Edge Seam

The edge to edge seam is useful when working with thicker knits, like *Tennessee* (see page 62), because it is almost invisible and forms no ridge thereby cutting down on unnecessary bulk. To work the seam place the pieces to be joined edge to edge, matching the pieces carefully row for row or, as on shoulders, stitch for stitch. Then, using the main colour, sew into the *head* of each stitch alternately.

Backstitch Seam

The backstitch seam is a strong, firm seam which is suitable for most garments but forms a ridge. Place the pieces to be joined together with right sides facing. Carefully match any colour patterns row for row or stitch for stitch. Work backstitch along the seam close to the edge, sewing into the centre of each stitch or row to correspond with the stitch or row on the opposite piece.

CARE AND MAINTENANCE

Most of the yarns recommended for the designs in this book are made up of natural fibres – cotton, wool or mohair. With the exception of cotton natural fibres should be treated with care and hand washed. Considering the work that has gone into knitting a garment, it would be extremely upsetting to ruin it by thoughtless aftercare.

Wool and Mohair

Although you should always refer to the yarn label for washing instructions for wool and mohair yarns, as a general rule these fibres can be hand washed gently in lukewarm water using a mild detergent.

Never allow natural fibres to soak as this may result in colour loss and too much time in detergent will attack the fibres anyway. Do not lift the garment while wet as the weight of the water will pull it out of shape. Instead, gently squeeze the water out before rinsing and rinse again until the water runs clear. If you have a short spin cycle on your washing machine, it is possible to spin the excess water out to reduce the drying time – but again use care. *Do not hang* the garment to dry, but instead dry it flat on a towel after you have laid it out and smoothed it gently into shape.

If washing has flattened your mohair knitting, the fibres can be teased to fluff them out by using a soft bristle brush and very light strokes so as not to pull out the stitches.

Cotton and Cotton Den-m-nit

Again, for cotton yarns refer to the yarn label for care instructions, especially for Rowan *Den-m-nit Indigo Dyed Cotton*. Cotton does not have to be treated with quite as much caution as wool and therefore it is possible to wash cottons in the washing machine on a gentle cycle. The addition of fabric conditioner when washing cotton will keep it soft to the touch.

Rown *Den-m-nit Indigo Dyed Cotton* possesses the same unique features as denim jeans. It will shrink and fade as it is worn and washed. The dye loss will be the greatest during the initial wash. The appearance of the garment will, however, be greatly enhanced with additional washing. It should be washed in the washing machine using fabric conditioner and tumble dried.

Please note that when knitting with this type of denim yarn the dye occasionally comes off onto the knitters hands. The colouring is removed easily but may 'smudge' onto other fabrics it comes into contact with before it has been washed and dried the first time.

KNITTING ABBREVIATIONS

alt	alternate(ly)	**RS**	right side(s)
approx	approximately	**sl**	slip
beg	begin(ning)	**st(s)**	stitch(es)
cm	centimetre(s)	**st st**	stocking
cn	cable needle		(stockinette)
cont	continu(e)(ing)		stitch
dec	decreas(e)(ing)	**tbl**	through back
foll	follow(s)(ing)		of loop(s)
g	gramme(s)	**tog**	together
inc	increas(e)(ing)	**WS**	wrong side(s)
K	knit	**yd**	yard(s)
LH	left hand	**yo**	yarn over
m	metre(s)		(needle)
mm	millimetre(s)		
oz	ounce(s)		
P	purl		
patt	pattern		
psso	pass slip stitch over		
rem	remain(s)(ing)		
rep	repeat(ed)(ing)		
rev st st	reverse stocking (stockinette) st		
RH	right hand		

ACKNOWLEDGEMENTS

Again we would like to say many thanks to everyone who has been involved in this book.
To Kathleen Hargreaves and everyone at Rowan. To Trisha Mackensie at Patons. To Jaeger, Wendy and Twilleys yarns.
To Shirley Jones and her team of knitters. To Florence Cowood, Betty Kennedy, Joan Eve, Phyllis and Rachael Kingman for their lovely work knitting up the designs. To Trevor Leighton, of course, for his wonderful photographs. To Sharon Lewis (stylist), who has joined Sally Harding (editor) as joint holder for the most efficient person in the Western Hemisphere. To Rick Haylor and Charlie Duffy who both did superb work on hair and make-up with our gorgeous models Sharon Henry and Jane Crossley. To Ruth Crafer, Tervor's thoughtful assistant, who was in charge of the grub, a vital part of the photo session.
To Bet Ayer for the design of the book and Textype for the charts. To Marilyn Wilson for her pains taking pattern checking. Not only, but also, a very big thank you to Valerie Buckingham at Ebury who has always been so enthusiastic about 'Big Knits'.

YARN AND KIT INFORMATION

BUYING YARN

Whenever possible it is best to use the yarn specified in the knitting pattern instructions. Contact the addresses on page 112 for information on your nearest stockist. When ordering a specific yarn, specify the colour by the shade number rather than the colour name.

If you wish to purchase a substitute yarn, choose a yarn of the same type and the same weight as the recommended yarn. The descriptions (below) of the various yarns used in the book can be used as a guide to the yarn weight and type (i.e. cotton, mohair, wool, et cetera). When purchasing a substitute yarn, calculate the amount needed by the number of metres (yards) required rather than by the number of grammes (ounces). When in doubt ask your yarn shop for assistance in substituting one yarn for another.

Jaeger *Matchmaker Sport* (100% pure new wool)
approx 75m (82yd) per 50g (1¾oz) ball

Jaeger *Pure Cotton Double Knitting* (100% cotton)
approx 112m (122yd) per 50g (1¾oz) ball

Patons *Fashion Mohair* (76% mohair/15% wool/9% nylon)

approx 98m (107yd) per 50g (1¾oz) ball

Patons *Classic Cotton DK* (100% mercerized cotton)
approx 112m (122yd) per 50g (1¾oz) ball

Rowan *Den-m-nit Indigo Dyed Cotton DK* (100% cotton)
approx 93m (102yd) per 50g (1¾oz) ball

Rowan *Chunky Cotton Chenille* (100% cotton)
approx 140m (153yd) per 100g (3½oz) hank

Rowan *Chunky Fox Tweed* (100% pure new wool)
approx 100m (109yd) per 100g (3½oz) hank

Rowan *Handknit DK Cotton* (100% cotton)
approx 85m (90yd) per 50g (1¾oz) ball

Twilleys *Pegasus* (100% cotton)
approx 150m (164yd) per 100g (3½oz) hank

Wendy *Capri DK* (51% cotton/49% acrylic)
approx 105m (115yd) per 50g (1¾oz) ball

Wendy *Orinoco DK* (60% acrylic/20% alpaca/20% nylon)
approx 162m (177yd) per 50g (1¾oz) ball

Note *Double knitting yarn (DK) is equivalent in weight to a heavy sport weight or a light knitting worsted weight in the U.S.A. 'Chunky' yarn is a 'bulky' weight in the U.S.A.*

KNITTING KITS
All of the designs in the book are available as Knitting Kits by mail order from Melinda Coss, Tyrwaun Bach, Gwernogle, Nr Brechfa, Dyfed, West Wales. Tel: 0267 202 386.

SYLVIE SOUDAN READY TO WEAR
Sylvie Soudan's ready to wear range is now available by mail order. For further details send a large self addressed envelope to 'Big Knits', 5 Clifton Road, London W9 1SZ, England.

ACCESSORIES
The clothes in the book come from '1647', a shop in London set up by Helen Teague and Dawn French for big beautiful girls. Tel: (071) 483 0733.

The jewellery is from The Outlaws Club, 49 Endell Street, London WC2.

YARN ADDRESSES

Most of the yarns used are widely available in yarn shops. For local and international stockists, please contact the manufacturers and distributors listed below.

Note *Although every effort is made to ensure that each yarn was available at the time of publication, it is not possible to guarantee that a yarn manufacturer will not change its yarn range. The yarns used, however, are all standard weights (see page 111 for how to find a substitute yarn).*

JAEGER AND PATONS YARNS
For information on stockists in the United Kingdom contact the following:

UK: Patons and Baldwins Ltd, PO Box 10, Alloa, Clackmannanshire, Scotland. Tel: 0259 723431

Availability of Jaeger and Patons yarns outside the United Kingdom varies from country to country and information about availability can be obtained from the following distributors:

Australia: Coats Patons Crafts, 89-91 Peters Avenue, Mulgrave, Victoria 3170. Tel: (3) 561 2288

Canada: Coats Patons Inc, 1001 Roselawn Avenue, Toronto, Ontario M6B 1B8. Tel: (416) 782 4481

New Zealand: Coats Patons (New Zealand) Ltd, Box 51-645, 263 Ti Rakau Drive, Pakuranga, Auckland. Tel: (9) 274 0021

U.S.A.: Coats and Clark Inc, 30 Patewood Drive, Suite 351, Greenville, SC 29615. Tel: (803) 234 0331

ROWAN YARNS
For information on stockists in the United Kingdom and the rest of Europe contact the following:

UK: Rowan Yarns, Green Lane Mill, Holmfirth, West Yorkshire, England HD7 1RW. Tel: (0484) 681881

For information on availability of Rowan yarns outside the United Kingdom contact the following distributors:

Australia: Sunspun Enterprises Pty Ltd, 191 Canterbury Road, Canterbury, Victoria 3126. Tel: (03) 830 1609

Canada: Estelle Designs and Sales Ltd, Units 65/67, 2220 Midland Avenue, Scarborough, Ontario M1P 3E6. Tel: (416) 298 9922

Ireland: Needlecraft, 27/28 Dawson Street, Dublin 2. Tel: (01) 772493

New Zealand: John Q. Goldingham Ltd, PO Box 45083, Epuni Railway, Lower Hutt. Tel: (04) 5674 085

USA: Westminster Trading Corporation, 5 Northern Boulevard, Amherst, NH 03031. Tel: (603) 886 5041

TWILLEYS YARNS
For information on stockists in the United Kingdom contact the following:

UK: Twilleys of Stamford Ltd, Roman Mill, Stamford, Lincolnshire PE9 1BG. Tel: 0780 52661

Twilleys *Pegasus* is not available outside the UK. (See page 111 for how to find a substitute yarn.)

WENDY YARNS
For information on stockists in the United Kingdom contact the following:

UK: Carter & Parker Ltd, Netherfield Road, Guiseley, West Yorkshire LS20 9PD. Tel: 0943 72264

For information on availability of Wendy yarns outside the United Kingdom contact the following distributors:

Australia: TCW Pty Ltd, 30 Guess Avenue, Arncliffe, New South Wales 2205. (02) 597 2955 and (02) 597 7573

Canada: R Stein Yarn Corporation Ltd, 303-5800 St Denis Street, Montreal H2S 3L5. Tel: (514) 274 9475

New Zealand: Wendy Wools (NZ) Ltd, PO Box 13176, Onehunga, Auckland. Tel: 9-640601

U.S.A.: Berroco Inc, Elmdale Road, PO Box 367, Uxbridge, MA 01569. Tel: (508) 278 2527